Spinning Straw Into Gold

The Art of Creating Money

Limited Preview Edition

Communion of Light Book of Ideas Series

Spinning Straw Into Gold: The Art of Creating Money

Loving What You Do ~ Doing What You Love
(coming soon)

Your Helpers
(coming soon)

Spinning Straw Into Gold
The Art of Creating Money

A Communion of Light Book of Ideas
Limited Preview Edition

Frank W. Butterfield

Butterfield Imprint
MMXII

ISBN-10: 1463571410
ISBN-13: 978-1463571412

First publication: September 2012

Note: This is not a book about financial planning. Please consult a competent financial planning professional before making any important financial decisions.

Printed in the United States of America.

Love never ends.

Table of Contents

Preface

Well, hello there!

Thank you for buying this Limited Preview Edition of *Spinning Straw Into Gold: The Art of Creating Money*.

As I write this, it's a cloudy warm Friday at the end of August. I am sitting in a Starbucks on Highway 71, southwest of Austin, Texas. A cover of Fleetwood Mac's *Gypsy* is playing overhead and a man at the table behind me is having a very intense business meeting over the phone. In other words, it's just a normal day.

And, I'm having trouble writing these words coherently because something wonderful has just happened. I have just had a brilliant, mad-cap, and completely unreasonable idea that is really zinging: let's print this book before it's really done!

There are so many reasons why this really should not happen. So many very good, very rational, very right reasons.

And, yet, the way this book even came into being happened because of a series of brilliant, mad-cap, and completely unreasonable ideas and actions on the part of myself and others. So, in a way, it makes a lot of sense.

But, in truth, I am just following what this very book suggests. I am paying attention to my intuition by following what feels better to me and trusting that this is leading me exactly where I want to go.

As you read this book, and ponder the unusual and somewhat revolutionary (yet often written and discussed, if not actually applied) ideas inside, I highly recommend that you ponder if there is something brilliant, mad-cap, and completely unreasonable that is rising up within you.

It might just be a whole heck of a lot of fun to go in that direction. And you might very well be surprised to discover that it leads you right where you want to go.

You see, that's the difference between making money and creating money, which is what the heart of this book is all about.

I don't know about you, but when I was making money, I was all about being reasonable and level-headed and trying to appear normal. In other words, I was trying to be that square peg in the proverbial round hole. And it really didn't work out that well.

But now I'm all about creating money, thanks to my very handsome non-physical friends who speak through me and are known as Paul. And life is much better. And getting better all the time.

I invite you to read what they have to say about this subject of creating money, or as they call it: spinning straw into gold.

I also invite you to take what works for you, what sings to you, what feels better to you, and to make it your own. Don't worry about trying to understand every single paragraph of this book. You'll know which parts are specifically for you because they will stand out and reading the words will be very sweet.

So, thank you again for purchasing this book. It was a delicious journey to bring it to you and one that continues.

It is my heart-felt desire and intention that you find the words you read in this book to be immensely helpful in every way possible that is inspirational, uplifting, illuminating, practical, and useful. I don't think that's too much to ask, do you?

With much love and appreciation,

Frank Butterfield
Austin, Texas, USA
August 31, 2012

What this book is and how to read it

This is a channeled book. The contents have been edited from transcripts.

What this means in practical terms is that for 21 days, I hosted daily recorded conversations each morning via a conference call on the topic of Spinning Straw Into Gold and specifically on the ideas listed in the Table of Contents.

During these conversations, I went into a slightly altered state of consciousness end entered into a session with the Communion of Light, allowing them to speak through me using a single voice known as Paul.

Paul & The Communion of Light are a collection of non-physical entities who speak consistently about the truth of who we are as the creators of the very specific reality we live in.

Paul speaks through me, using my voice and my inner English-language translator and the vocabulary in my consciousness.

They speak of themselves in the plural, using words such as "we," "us," and "our."

One of my very best friends, whom I've known for many years and who is a bit skeptical about all of this channeled stuff, says that Paul speaks like me, using my language and idioms.

And, I would agree with that assessment. only I think he is giving me more credit than I deserve. I'm often quite surprised by the precision, insight, and wit they display in conversation.

Also, they are infinitely more focused and patient in bringing home a point than I am ever capable of being in conversation, particularly with people who don't necessarily agree with the point to start off with.

Whether you agree with my friend or if you just aren't quite sure about the concept of channeled material, it might help to think of this material as coming from a place of broader and more expanded awareness from within me, using a way of communicating that is different from my normal, waking method of expressing myself.

This book is not a workbook.

It does not contain worksheets, techniques, or processes, although you could certainly create many wonderful ones from the contents.

This book contains a collection of ideas on the radical topic of creating money, and looks at them, comparing them to the more usual idea of making money.

The flow and contents of this book are designed to stimulate ideas within you that are specific to where you are in relationship to these topics.

There are several ways to read this book.

One way would be to read it from start to finish. That could be very satisfying and help you develop the powerful idea of creating money in a systematic way.

Another way would be to read a chapter at a time and allow the ideas to steep a bit before moving on to the next one. That could be very illuminating over time.

You could also hold a question in mind, open the book to a random page, and notice the first words that jump out at you. This could be very surprising and transformational, depending on whether you are wanting either.

Finally, you could clear your mind, open the book anywhere, and begin reading with the intention of profoundly expanding your own personal idea of abundance. That could be very delicious!

Prologue

We've spoken of the difference between making money and creating money.

Let us go a little bit deeper into the distinction between the two.

When you are making money, essentially what you are doing: you are creating for yourself, in very specific ways, the avenues by which actions that you take will result in the receiving of money or remuneration in some way for what you have done.

It's quite simple.

You have an idea.

You take that idea and you put it into action.

And as a result of your action, money comes to you.

So, for example, you might be drawn to selling something that someone else you know is making.

And you say: "All right, I will take your thing, and I will turn around and I will sell it in the marketplace. And for the benefit of my service of selling, I will take a certain percentage of what it is that is being sold for the effort that I am putting into the selling."

And this might come as a result of an idea that you had, feeling as though this is something that would feel very good to you to sell, that you would like to sell it, that you would find great pleasure in selling it, or that you think it would be easy to sell.

In other words, the organizing principle of all thought is bringing you the path of least resistance for what it is that you are wanting to experience.

Similarly, when you are working for someone else and they are paying you, and there is a contract for what you are doing, and you have agreements about the nature of your employment or the nature of your work, and that sort of thing, you build within yourself a very powerful expectation of being paid for your work, and being paid in a way that you are in agreement with.

You might not like everything about what you are experiencing; but let it be very clear that you are indeed creating that very specific circumstance.

So, in this way, you are making money.

You are doing something, thinking something, saying something, acting upon something, coordinating events, bringing things together in ways that feel good to you, or that feel manageable, or that feel doable, that are within reach.

Not all of it may seem obvious from every single moment.

In other words, there may be an unfolding story where things get better and better, or easier and easier, or more in alignment.

And alignment doesn't necessarily always feel really good, but alignment feels very powerful.

And you can be swimming upstream very hard, and still be in alignment with something.

Because you've said: "No matter what, I'm going to make this happen. No matter what, I am going to do this."

And so, that "no matter what" may mean going upstream.

From the point of your decision where you said: "This is what I will have. This is what I will do. I will make this money. I will do it in this way, and this is what will work for me," you are drawing to you more and more of whatever you are bringing your emphasis to.

If that is your decision, and that is your focus, and that is your way of thinking, then you will receive evidence supporting what you are noticing.

In this way, the organizing principle is neutral.

It does not try to get you to go in a certain direction.

It doesn't try to turn you.

You may have a mixed vibration about what you are doing, and therefore may receive multiple signals: one saying go right, another one saying go left: things that are obviously contradictory to each other.

But, that is just a reflection of the thoughts that you are thinking.

It is not some sort of invisible hand in the sky trying to direct you in a certain direction.

You are indeed guiding yourself in this way.

You are the one who is drawing to you all the methods and manners and processes and resources that reinforce the ideas of what you are focusing on when you are making money.

Your inner direction is the most powerful tool that you have at your disposal.

What feels better to you—what feels like relief—is going to be going in the direction of what you want more of.

And that's the simplest way to work through these things that seem to be contradictory.

But what we really want you to understand is that there is no hidden hand; there is no man sitting on a chair up in the sky with a long beard who is directing you or guiding you.

There is no universe that is like a person that has an ax to grind in your life, that wants you to go in this direction or that direction.

There is nothing that is teaching you anything, or trying to give you lessons, or trying to show you this is the best way, this is the way that is the best for all concerned.

You may summon forth those experiences based upon your own thinking and your own beliefs.

And whatever you believe about these things, you will be right about.

You will gather evidence to you naturally, the organizing principle being neutral in this way.

It brings you more of whatever it is that you believe, and brings you more and more of it, as you get more and more entrenched in that thought.

This may be a thought that you like, and this may be a thought that you don't like.

Whichever. It doesn't really matter.

If you persist in thinking thoughts that you don't like, you will persist in receiving information and support and evidence and proof and further new thoughts about what you don't like.

The more you focus on anything, the more you will have thoughts about it, and then those thoughts will become experiences.

So, when you follow what feels better within the realm of making money, what begins to happen is that things get a lot easier usually.

Sometimes you may come up against things that have been there but you weren't quite aware of them, and you may feel as though you've tripped, or you've stumbled, or you've fallen off of the wagon or whatever it is that you may think about that.

But really all that's ever happening when you're following what feels better is you're going in the direction of the totality of your desires.

Your inner being holds an ideal vision, an ideal version of everything that you are wanting.

If you pay attention to the thoughts that feel better, the directions that feel better, the words that feel better in their speaking, and the actions that feel better in their doing, these things will lead you to the ultimate goal of what you are always wanting on any given topic, and even a mixture of topics that seem to be all blended together as one.

In the arena of making money, so often what happens is you get on a track and you decide: "This is what I will do, and I will do it come hell or high water."

And so here comes the hell, and here comes the high water.

And yet you persist, and you keep going, and you keep going, and you keep going, and you keep going.

And you make sure that you keep doing it, keep doing it, keep doing it.

And your powerful alignment, because of the nature of who you are, will eventually bring about the thing that you're wanting.

But there is a much easier way, which is to just flow with what you are wanting, and allow it to reveal to you the next thing, and the next thing, and the next thing, and the next thing.

But it does require trust in your outcome, or at least a little bit of willingness to trust that what you are wanting will actually come to you.

So often, if you are rowing upstream very hard, and you are working very hard to make something happen, what you are actually doing is saying: "I do not believe that I can have what I want, so I must go out and prove to myself that I can actually have it."

That is, for many people, the underlying vibration of such an effort, of such a strain.

We invite you to think about how your life can be

easy.

We invite you to think about how your life can be rich, how your life can be luscious, how your life can be delicious, how your life can be joyful, how your life can be filled with happy experiences and delightful synchronicities.

We invite you to think those thoughts because you will then have more and more of those experiences.

And as you find the things that feel better amongst all of those different thoughts, and you begin to follow them, what then begins to happen is that things begin to sort themselves out.

And, for those desires that you've had for long periods of time, but have felt as though you haven't quite ever made any progress on them, once you've stopped trying to make progress, what eventually begins to happen is that you begin to see signs of land; and then you begin to feel as though you're right on track, right on target with it.

So, when you are making money, the training that you've most likely received says: "There is a plan. And you must work the plan. And you must follow the plan, and you must do what the plan says. Because the plan will guide you."

When you are doing such a thing, you are turning off your own internal, native guidance.

You are ignoring.

You are saying: "I will not pay attention to how I am feeling. I will pay attention to the plan. I will pay attention to the words that either I wrote down in the past, or that someone else has prescribed for me. And I will follow this plan. And I will row upstream, and I will work really hard to make sure that I follow this plan and I do everything that is written out."

Now, it's quite possible that you could summon forth a plan where someone else writes it out for you, or you write it out for yourself, that feels really, really good to you, that really gives you what it is that you're wanting, and sends you right on your way downstream.

That's quite possible.

But we know, for the majority of you, that's not really where you start off.

So when you are in the process of making money, you may be out in the marketplace on your own selling "this," selling "that,"or you may be working for someone else, or with someone else, or for a company, or for an organization.

But if you are in the habit of taking action and then expecting money in return for the action, then you've got things defined in a way that for some might feel very secure and might feel very clear; but for others might, after a while, begin to feel very limiting.

And it is to those that we want to speak about the difference between making money and creating money.

1. The difference between making money and creating money

There is a vast difference in metaphysical approach between the idea of creating money and the idea of making money.

What we notice in our physical friends is that when you are going about the task of making money, you are focused on making something happen not for the joy of it—not for what it is that you are really wanting—but because in some way or another you are fulfilling a need or a desire that you yourself have either decided you have, or have agreed with others that you have.

So that is why many of you will come to us and say, "What is really my life's purpose? This can't be everything that I'm supposed to be about."

And for many of you it's because you're quite accustomed to making money.

And we don't mean—when we say that you're making money—that you're making money by working in a job, necessarily, where you are employed by someone else.

What we mean is that no matter what you're doing —whether you're working for yourself or working for someone else—the task before you is to make money, and you have associated making money with the idea of producing something.

Now, this is very obvious if you just look around and see.

In fact, it might make a lot of sense; and you might be thinking, "Well, so what's new here?"

The reason why we're bringing out this distinction is because—when you are making money and you are focused on completing the task and getting it done, and you are focused on looking at the results and doing what needs to be done now in order to have things work out later and in the most basic way—the way this works is that you are showing up to work and punching the time clock so that in two weeks you will receive your paycheck.

In other words, and in its most basic sense, when you are making money you are delaying the experience of what you are wanting.

Now, if you are in the process of making money, and if you are working at a job and you are making money or you are employing yourself and you are making money, your hackles might have been raised by now, and we would certainly understand why.

Because we're not telling you, "Don't punch that time clock, don't go to work, don't work on your projects, don't produce your widgets or deliver your services."

We're not saying that whatsoever.

What we're suggesting is, no matter where you are —no matter what you are doing, no matter what job you find yourself in, no matter what situation you find yourself in, whether you have a job or don't have a job, whether you're working for yourself or whether you consider yourself to be unemployed—you can change the way that you are approaching the dynamic of money, and start creating money instead of making money.

So, when you are creating money what you are doing is you are saying, "Right here, right now is where I will have the thing that I'm wanting."

And if you understand that the thing that you were wanting begins first with the vibration and then begins to manifest itself into physical form—whether it's in the next few seconds or minutes or hours or days or weeks or months or years, depending upon the resistance that you have to what it is that you are wanting—but if you understand that the point of creating money is so that you are in alignment with yourself, this is the single most important alignment that we would recommend that you seek.

You can certainly come into alignment with lots of different ideas—and, when we say alignment, what we mean is that you can bring yourself to a place vibrationally where you see the perfection of this or you see the rightness of it, or you find yourself feeling as though you are in the right place at the right time with the right thing, and you can do this at any time, at any place, with anyone, anywhere.

But what we're suggesting is that, first and foremost, you're going to want to find alignment with your Self—meaning your Inner Being, your Higher Self, the Source that dwells within you—because you are an extension of that Source Energy that dwells within you, and nothing is more important than your relationship with that Source.

In fact, everything else flows from it.

So, when you line up with the topic of money by realizing that you can create money—which means that you are removing the topic of money from the limitations of situation and circumstance—then you're liberating yourself to have as much money as you're wanting to have at any time that you can imagine.

What you will find, first and foremost, is that you're primarily aligning yourself with You.

When you bring money into that vortex relationship that you have with your Inner Being—your Higher Self—everything about your relationship with money will begin to change.

But this is a conscious decision that you must make if you are wanting to make it.

This is not something for most of you, because of the ways in which you have been taught by your culture.

This is not something that will just naturally arise without a little bit of effort—although not a whole great deal.

We're not just suggesting long periods of meditation or visualization or anything like that—although you might find those very, very helpful.

But what we are suggesting is that today—right now, as you go through the day—you can begin to imagine and ask yourself the question: "Am I making money here or am I creating money?"

Now, let us be clear.

There's nothing wrong with making money.

You're not doing anything wrong if you're approaching it in this way.

But if you are interested in learning how to master the art of creating money, and if you are interested in discovering your own innate ability to spin straw into gold—for you each have this ability—then you're probably going to want to turn your attention away from the thing that you've been doing in order to make money, and turn your attention towards all of the ways in which you can create money—and there are many, many ways in which you can do this.

In fact, there are an infinite number of ways in which whatever it is that you're wanting—money included—can come to you easily and effortlessly.

But you do have to decide that this is possible.

And so, in mastering the art of creating money, that is what you will be doing:

You will be letting go of the idea that money is tied to situation, circumstance, and even to people; and you will be turning your attention towards more open and broader ways of looking at and relating to money; and you will be bringing money into your vortex with your Inner Being—and we think that's a very, very delicious thing indeed.

So, as you continue this journey with us, you're going to discover how you are indeed already a master manifestor, and you're going to discover how you are indeed already creating wondrously delicious things for yourself in your experience of this physical world that you inhabit.

And we invite you to decide that you can live from the power of the present moment, leaning forward into the delicious future that you are creating.

We invite you to begin to imagine all of the things that you are wanting that will become easier and easier to have once you understand how you are already a master of manifestation and a powerful creator and that you can create money whenever it is that you are wanting.

So, as you go through this day today, we do invite you to look at the ways in which you are currently making money.

There's nothing wrong with what you are doing, but it might be helpful to become aware of these things, to make some notes either mentally or on a piece of paper, and to begin to notice, "Is this something that feels good?"

14

And just ask that question. "Does it feel good to be making money in the way that I am?"

Again, there's nothing right or wrong—just an inquiry.

2. Noticing how much money there is all around you

We invite you to ask yourself the question, "Where does money come from?"

Now, there are lots of things in your life that you take for granted, regardless of where the thing comes from, and one of the examples that we always like to discuss in this topic is the idea of hot and cold running water.

For, most of you—if not all of you—have that experience going on in your house right now as we speak, but you never really stop to think or wonder or worry about where is the next drop of water going to come from, and that is because you have a powerful expectation—a very powerful expectation—that the hot and cold running water in your house will be there when you want it; and in those rare occasions when it is not, you have such a strong desire to have the situation put back to normal

17

that it gets fixed quite quickly.

Now, we want you to think about money in the same way as you think about running water: that money is something that really you can turn off and turn on as much as you want, and there is an endless amount of it available to you.

What you might want to also think about is that—unlike hot and cold running water, which is metered and paid for—that, as for money—being just the form that energy takes in a very specific way—there is an unlimited amount of it.

There is an unlimited amount of money.

The only thing that limits your ability to receive money—to create money for your own use in the ways that you want to, in the ways that feel better to you—is literally your imagination.

So, if you could, imagine that your hot and cold running water was actually plugged into the ocean, and was treated and filtered and made nice for you in just the right sort of way, and that you really could literally leave the tap running all the time, because it would just circulate.

Water that you didn't use would find its way back into the ocean.

And it would normally and automatically clean itself and become more of what it is by your use of it.

So, what we want you to think about and what we want you to understand is that there is virtually an unlimited amount of money available to you; and as you go out through the day today, we want you to take a look around and look at all of the things that you can see in your physical environment that came about because of the exchange and use of money.

So, for example, if you were to go to the top of a hill and look out over the city that you live in, imagine what is the value of all of the buildings that you can see, and try to see if you can figure out how much money you can actually see in manifestation in the form of buildings.

The point here isn't really necessarily to get you to think about real estate; the point here is for you to notice that within a few hundred feet, if not an actual mile of you, there is a lot of money in manifested form.

Now, we know it's distributed among lots of different people, so we're not saying that magically somehow this becomes yours just because you can see it.

What we are saying is that when you notice something, you become more attuned to it; your vibration goes in that direction.

And we suggest that from this day forward, as you are continuing to learn how to spin straw into gold—as you're doing so very beautifully already—and as you're mastering the art of creating money, we suggest that you begin to realize that with your eyes you can see a lot more than probably what you have ever noticed before.

As you're driving around your town in your car, on the roads paved by the city that you live in, just notice what is all around you and all of the money that was involved in lighting the streets and paving the roads and building the cars and selling the cars, all the buildings and the sidewalks that were laid down, all the trees that were planted and all the trees that were preserved.

Everything around you was constructed in some way and built upon money.

Now, what's very, very delicious about this is, if you begin to become aware of how much abundance there is surrounding you, you're going to begin to notice how much abundance there is already in your own life if you will allow that to happen.

Another very juicy thing that will begin to occur is that you will notice all of the ways in which you are not particularly happy about the different people around you that have more money or access to more money according to your lights than you.

This is always a very, very good thing to be aware of, because that contrasting thought—where what you're doing is saying, "They have it but I don't"—that's something that you want to become aware of, because that's a thought that you want to allow to evolve.

If you will notice it and allow yourself to feel it—rather than pushing it away or trying to make yourself be more spiritually correct by not noticing it—but if you will allow yourself to realize, that thought actually has been extremely helpful, because you have launched many rockets of desire every time that you have thought, "I don't have this thing that I want, but they do."

What you're noticing now, from this place of intentional and deliberate creation, is that this thought is no

2. Noticing how much money there is all around you

longer useful and it's no longer helpful, because it doesn't really plug you into the vibration that you want to be in: one of expanded, freedom-centered abundance.

As you go through the day and you're noticing these things, you're paying attention to how—very specifically and very beautifully—money has been flowing through just the local economy that surrounds you: it paved the road, it built the cars, it planted the trees, it preserves the trees, it built the houses, it built the buildings.

Now, money itself didn't do any of these things; but money was used in the manifestation of these things, and that is its only purpose: it is part of the manifestation process.

It is not the only part, but it is a part that you obviously, from your attention to the subject, are wanting to be more and more integrated with on deeper and more profound levels.

So, today's role for you—and our suggestion at least —is to pay attention to the abundance that surrounds you.

Notice how you feel about it; and when you notice contrast—when you are aware of the fact that you want something but you don't have it, or you want something and they have it but you don't—to honor that by saying, "Yes, that was helpful once upon a time to be aware of that. Now I can feel that and allow that thought to evolve through me."

And then you will be free from that idea.

So, as you're moving forward, what we want you to

understand is that this place that you're in and that you're noticing—and this is probably the more radical step, more radical than anything we've said so far—the radical step is going to be to realize that what you see, you yourself have created.

Now, we know for some of you, you're not going to really like that idea very much.

Others will feel the freedom that is inherent in that idea.

But if you are noticing that this idea feels like a contracting place to you, we would invite you to think about the very nature of your reality and how things are arranged around you.

You don't have to agree with us on this topic, by the way. You don't have to believe in any of the things that we're saying at all, in fact.

What we would recommend—more importantly than you believing in anything that we assert—is to find the things that we're offering that feel very good to you, and that feel like an enhanced and expanded place from where you have been; and lock onto those, and feel them, and expand into them, and amplify them through your noticing.

It's not your job to line up with everything that we are saying.

What we're offering is the broadest possible and most expanded view of how you are already creating money; and what we suggest is that you allow those pieces and parts of what we're offering that feel very good to you and that really sing to you, to be the things that you use and take from this conversation.

So, as you're noticing your physical environment, and as you're beginning to ask yourself the question, "Where did all of this money come from?" what we want you to understand is that at the very basis of all of this—at the bottom of it all—is that it came from you.

You are Source Energy in manifestation, and as you master the art of creating money, you will begin to understand that everything you are summoning forth is available to you; and the reason why it is available to you is for no other reason than you are Source Energy in manifestation.

You have taken on the guise of the personality that you have generated for yourself, using the name that you call yourself by, and everything that you experience you have drawn to you.

So this is a really wonderful opportunity to begin to fine-tune and define and refine what it is that you're wanting more of from where you are right now.

And this day, as you're walking around taking note —noticing how much money there is already around you, how much money you have already summoned forth into your experience—even if you don't have it in your hot little hands right at this moment, it's still surrounding you—we invite you to notice these things, and we invite you to allow the contrast that will arise from this noticing to simply evolve.

Realize it's not a big deal.

You have some old thoughts that were helpful once upon a time but now are ready to go, and you can let them go.

You might have to feel a little bit of what the feeling is, but that's okay too, because it's not going to be the end of things.

In fact, it will be the beginning.

And that's a very, very good place to be, indeed.

3. Your imagination is your most powerful tool

There is within you a broad and vast power—one that has been with you since the beginning of All That Is, and one that you are using and drawing upon constantly, even if you do not know that you are using it.

This singular power is what you are using to literally sculpt the reality in which you exist.

All of the content and the context that you see surrounding you—that you feel in your presence when you look through your physical eyes and you look out onto a physical world—all of this has come into being because of one thing and one thing alone: your imagination.

Your ability to imagine what it is that you are wanting is what allows you to create everything that you are creating, including something as simple as the ability to walk across the room and move from one chair to another.

What we want you to understand today is that, as you are imagining, what you are doing is you are literally pulling together the very threads of reality, and you are weaving the new pattern, the new texture, and the new context that you are wanting to experience, moment after moment.

Now, we could say it is your thoughts that are creating reality—and that certainly is the case—but we're using the word imagination, because isn't imagination really a concert of thinking: a harmonious, beautiful choir of delicious thoughts that are singing in unison and creating a context and content—creating not only the experience, but the place in which the experience happens and the ways in which the experience occurs, and what it feels like and what it looks like and how it sounds, what it tastes like, what it smells like, what it feels like to be physically present in that experience.

It is a whole concert of thinking that happens in unison, and you—the powerful master manifestor that you already are—are quite adept at doing this.

The wonderful thing is that you can realize that your ability to move from one chair to another in the same room is the exact same ability that allows you to create anything that you can possibly imagine.

You think that you understand how it is that each of these things that you are creating in your life is happening—and generally each of you thinks that it happens because of what you do—but in fact it happens because of what you imagine.

So, in the example of moving across the room from

one chair to another, you have to decide that what you are going to do is actually change your location, and that you're going to move from that one chair to the other chair.

Your body then follows you, according to the Law of Attraction—that single organizing principle of the Universe that brings all of this together.

So, as you move across the room, your body is doing a whole series of complex actions involving muscles and tendons and your sense of gravity and your sense of touch, all of which move you across that room; but you are not actually doing the moving—not in the complex way that that movement is required in order to occur.

Rather, you're relying upon a series of expectations that you have—all of which is tied into your imagination.

When first you learned how to do this—when first you learned how to crawl across the floor, and then you learned how to pull yourself up, and then you learned how to walk across the floor, and then you learned how to run—all of these things happened because you had an imagination.

You could see someone else doing it, and you could imagine yourself doing it as well, and you had the desire and you had the drive and you had the desire.

Did we mention desire?

You had the desire to move yourself from one place to another; and thus it happened.

So, now, today, we want to invite you to imagine having what it is that you are wanting more of in terms of money.

But the important thing—like moving yourself from one chair to another across the room—is to see yourself having it in a way that is real for you.

If you are thinking about what you are wanting in terms of fluffy clouds and rainbows and things that could happen or might happen, but that you don't really believe can happen, it's all right to start there; but what you're going to want to do is to find some aspect of what you are imagining that is real and grounded and reflective of what you believe you are capable of having.

You don't need to know how to get there; and when we say making it real—when we say getting down into the reality of it, into the grounded reality of it—we don't mean figuring out how it's going to happen.

What we mean is you need to find a way to relate to the thing that you are imagining: this expanded self that is in a great place of abundance and prosperity in terms of money.

You need to find a way to see how that would happen in a way that is very real to you; again, not the method by which it happens, but the manner—what it feels like—what it feels like to be there, connected to the reality of this expanded wealth, increased money—whether it's more income or more just the plain experience of having more of what you're wanting.

So, this is a very good place to begin here today: to remember the power of your imagination and to notice all of the things that you are doing already here today that involve imagination, where you have to decide, "This is what I want and this is what I will have."

And you do this quite simply.

You do it by just picturing what it is that you are looking for, and then allowing yourself to bring yourself into the picture, seeing yourself having it in ways that are meaningful to you.

So, every time that you are about to prepare a meal, or every time you are about to move across the floor, or every time you are going to pick up the phone or you are going to type an email, there's always some sort of imagining that you are doing.

Most of it is so normal and so hum-drum that you don't really notice it; but today we invite you to notice all of the imagining that is going on, for there is quite a bit, and it is quite powerful, and it is what is fueling every single aspect of your physical reality.

It is this brilliant symphony that you have pulled together specifically for you—on your behalf—creating more of what you want; and just as you do so, day by day by day with all manner of things, so too can you do so with money.

The thing that you might be thinking is that it's a little bit more difficult, or it's a little bit thornier, because you don't quite have it and you're not quite there yet.

Well, today is the day to unleash your imagination —to unfetter what you believe is possible for you.

4. Everyone, everywhere, wants to help you

There is nothing at all—nothing at all, whatsoever —going on in your life, in your experience, in all that you have summoned to you, that is actually trying to keep you from having what you're wanting.

If you are going through your life and you are thinking about your relationship with money, and you are wondering why you don't have what it is that you are wanting, let us first say—and be unequivocal in it— that it's not because anyone or anything is blocking you from having the experience—and that includes your own mind.

The reason we say this is because we know that it's a very popular thing to discuss how your unconscious mind and your unconscious beliefs are betraying you or sabotaging you, and we want to bring this out on the table and look at it quite plainly.

As long as you believe and as long as you are thinking about sabotage and delay and betrayal, Law of Attraction—being what it is, that single organizing principle of the universe that brings you more of whatever it is that you focus upon—will prove that you are right.

You cannot clean up or clean out your unconscious mind enough; because, as you are doing that, you will find more and more things that need to be corrected or fixed or removed or released or healed or transformed.

So, we would rather you start at the beginning— and whether you do this or not is completely up to you, just as any of the things that we suggest here are completely up to you—but this is what we would suggest: that you start off by saying, "Everyone, everywhere wants to help me."

And we mean this quite literally—and everyone, everywhere includes you and all of the different parts and pieces of the puzzle that is you.

So, if you're being with that assumption that everyone, everywhere wants to help you, you will find that you are increasingly more and more right about that statement; because Law of Attraction—being what it is, that single organizing principle of the universe—will bring you evidence to prove your assertion that everyone, everywhere does indeed want to help you.

Now, when we say this, we don't mean that everyone, everywhere wants to help you with their own knowledge.

They're not sitting there thinking of ways to help you out.

What we mean by this is that when you assert this, what you're going to find is that people who otherwise would have been difficult and thoughts that otherwise would have been intransigent suddenly seem to shake loose and get a lot easier.

This doesn't mean that what you're doing is running around consciously controlling everything.

What it means, however, is that in the context of all that you are wanting, from that very dynamic perspective of everything that you are summoning forth through your powerful desires, everyone, everywhere does indeed want to help you.

The basis for this statement, metaphysically, is quite sound, and it's quite simple too.

The basis is just this: when you are flowing downstream, you are in alignment with your powerful desires; and your powerful desires, having emerged from the thoughts that you have been thinking, are absolutely and completely in alignment with the expansion and evolution of All That Is.

In short, what you are wanting is what Source Energy is wanting, and Source Energy is All That Is—and that includes you and the thoughts that you think.

It also includes all of the other people that inhabit the physical world of your creation.

So, to say that everyone, everywhere wants to help you is simply just a statement of fact; and what we mean by this is that Source Energy—being All That Is—is always wanting to help you in the downstream way.

Now, what you will not find is that anyone is ever—

and this has probably already been proven to you over and over again—is ever terribly interested in helping you push against yourself.

They may say that they are; but when you are rowing upstream, you're really just a party of one.

Yes, we understand that there are a vast number of cultural resources devoted quite specifically to helping you row upstream—meaning to do things the hard way, to do things because suffering is necessary, or suffering is an essential part of the story, or somehow or another you're supposed to work really, really hard to make things happen by efforting and striving and struggling.

But if you'll notice, every time you do that, no one really wants to help you with it.

However, when you let go and you float downstream, and you begin to allow the universe to carry you, it's quite simple: what you're doing is you're just following the next thought that feels better, speaking the next words that feel better to say in their saying, and following the next action that feels better to do in its execution.

When you are doing this, everyone, everywhere does indeed want to help you.

Now, we don't mean that they are saying they want to help you.

They may be actively resisting, because they themselves see value in rowing upstream.

They may be actively resisting whatever it is that you are about in their presence; but if you continuously are asserting to yourself—or at least with some regularity—the statement, "Everyone, everywhere wants to help me," well then, you're going to find proof of this, over and over again.

And you might indeed find that the most intransigent of people suddenly are more pliable and are more allowing of their own experience, which then allows them in their own way to be of service to you; just as when you are more pliable and allowing you are of infinitely more service to vast numbers of people.

It's amazing what you can contribute when you are allowing your own good and well-being to flow.

So, as you are thinking about money today, notice what it feels like to begin to assert that, "Everyone, everywhere wants to help me."

Notice the places where you believe this; notice the places where you don't believe it.

And it's okay if you don't believe it.

It's okay if you're thinking, "Well, this is just the biggest load of bull-hockey that I've ever heard."

That's completely fine.

We just invite you to go through the day today—particularly in the context of money, but in all areas of your life—and look around and notice, "Do I believe that everyone, everywhere wants to help me?"

And if you don't—if there's someplace where you think, "Well, yes, they generally do; but in this specific area they do not"—just take a moment to see if you could actually imagine something very different happening in that scenario.

Remember that you don't have to push hard; this

isn't a big deal, because eventually you will understand that everyone, everywhere does indeed want to help you—but it would be really nice to understand that sooner rather than later.

For when you croak—when you die, when you move on from this physical experience—it will become clear that Source Energy really is All That Is.

It's not All That Is minus this little pocket over here, or All That Is minus those people over there.

Source Energy—being a constantly flowing and expanding idea that encompasses All That Is and All that ever can be and All that ever has been—is in harmony with itself; and you are part and parcel of All That Is.

And it is impossible for you to not be in harmony with yourself.

You can pretend that you are not; you can act as though you are not; you can actively resist it; but it is still All That Is that is out in display right in front of you, including those people who you think are difficult or thorny or even impossible to be around or to work with or to play with.

So, as you go through your day today noticing how everyone, everywhere wants to help you, we invite you to just allow that statement to be more and more true.

Remember that it's not going to always look that way on the surface.

So, your job is to look past the surface things and remember the essence of what is happening here.

5. There is nothing that is limiting your ability to create what you want

There is no doubt at all—at least within us—that you are capable of anything that you decide you are capable of creating, becoming, having, or doing.

There really is no limit to what it is that you can conceive of; and whatever it is that you can conceive of is something that you can actually experience, have, do, or be.

We want to invite you today to start thinking more along these lines, and less about what it is that you do not have or cannot do or have not done.

When you begin to turn your attention to the potential—or what is coming, and the possibilities of what you are creating, and to the expanded version of the you that you are becoming—what happens is that you

37

begin to liberate yourself from the chains of the past, from the binds and the bounds that you have put upon yourself that keep you from believing in who you really are.

Well, you see, we have no doubt about who you are; and at the core of your being you certainly have no doubt about this either, but you have trained yourself vibrationally to believe that somehow you are less than who you are: perfect and whole, right now.

On the topic of money—on the topic of spinning straw into gold—knowing that anything is possible is the beginning of the realization that you can have what it is that you are wanting.

When we discussed earlier the difference between making money and creating money, what we noticed is that most of you who are making money are doing so because you believe that this is the only way that you can get your needs met, this is the only way that you can take care of business, this is the only way that you can guarantee that what you are wanting—at least a little tiny portion of it that you believe you can have—is going to actually come to you.

However, what we want you to understand is that when you are creating money, what you are doing is tapping into the infinite possibility, tapping into the infinite Source, tapping into the infinite abundance of All That Is.

There really is no limit to what you can create.

The only limitation that you ever have is the limitation that you place upon yourself.

No one is that interested in you, to keep you repressed from who you are.

Many well-intentioned people may be telling you, or have told you in the past, that if you think too big or dream too big that you're going to be disappointed, so it might be a better idea to stay close to home and keep things reasonable and moderated.

We understand why that certainly would feel better than the thought that you're living in a wildly chaotic universe.

But here we intend to go further.

We invite you to—as you go through this day—begin to imagine the biggest possible thing that you can imagine—whatever it may be—but particularly as it pertains to money.

We don't necessarily mean thinking about large sums of money, although that may be part of what you're wanting.

We invite you to just think big, no matter what the subject is, no matter how money is involved, whether you think money is necessary to have this or not.

It doesn't really matter.

We just invite you to think about and begin training yourself in the direction of a more expanded version of the you that you are becoming, particularly if you feel as though you are in a rut.

This exercise—for as long as you do it and with as much or as little gusto as you put into the experience—will help you realize that there are other possibilities.

You see, by engaging the Law of Attraction—the

single organizing principle of the universe—in this little theme of expanded thinking, what you are doing is drawing to you more and more thoughts, more and more ideas, and eventually—as you allow it to happen—more experiences, more situations, more people that align with the bigger vision, the expanded version.

In a way, we could say it is your destiny to become whatever it is that you are dreaming of.

That is why we have said to you that your imagination is your most powerful tool.

Do you want to be destined to a life where you feel as though there were missed opportunities or choices that you did not make that you could have made, or do you want to be destined for an expanding version of you?

There's no right or wrong answer to this question.

There are many good reasons—many good reasons—why you would want to do one over the other; but we suspect that if you really pay attention to what is going on within you, and notice the thoughts that you are thinking, and notice how you feel as you think these thoughts, you will find the more expanded thoughts to be more attractive thoughts.

You will find them to feel better for you.

As you explore what it means throughout the day to have an expanded vision—and as you think about what that would look like and what it would feel like to have whatever it is that you're dreaming of—we also invite you to pay attention to the fact that you really don't know how to get there, and see if you can be okay with that very simple fact.

You see, it's always true that you really don't know how to get from one place to another.

You think you do, from things that you've done over and over again, where it seems like the exact same thing happened, each step being the same along the way.

But remember, each moment is a new moment and you're never really doing the same thing twice.

This isn't just a metaphysical conceit or a philosophical truism; this is actually something that you can demonstrate by noticing that you are not exactly the same person that you were the last time you did something; and so if you are going to repeat it—let's say just the simple act of making a sandwich—you never really make the same sandwich twice, and you never really do exactly the same amount of this, that or the other.

And as true as that is for something as small as a sandwich, it's mostly true—in fact, it's more so true—in fact, it's absolutely true—for anything else that you might be imagining.

The wonderful thing is that you don't know how to get from here to there; and the wonderful thing is that since you do not know how to get there, you can train yourself—something that is quite natural for you to do if you allow it to happen—to be guided from here to there.

Now, this guidance is not like an unseen hand that is moving you.

This guidance is what naturally arises within you

when you decide, "I will be over there from here."

As soon as you decide, "This is what I will have," the way to get there is immediately established.

And no matter how you follow—whether you do it exactly the way it lays out for you as you do it, or whether you hem and haw and procrastinate and can't make up your mind and aren't quite sure and can't quite get there—it doesn't matter how long you delay it —every moment has within it the ability to lead you to exactly where you want to go.

There is no question that does not have an answer; and there is no destination that does not have a path to get there.

And when you realize that it is your imagining—it is your dreaming—it is your ability to think of something more than where you are right in the moment in manifested reality—that is actually causing all of the really wonderful, delicious experiences to come to you— they don't just happen randomly; they happen because you dreamed them into being—then we think that you're probably going to want to spend a lot more time dreaming about who you are becoming, and imagining what it is that is possible, and feeling your way into the deliciousness of those possibilities, and beginning to notice how they are real more than they are not.

We think that, as you do this, you are going to feel a connection that you have to that creative power that is within you—and this is your ability to literally spin straw into gold.

For what is the straw but just the raw building

blocks?

It's just the potential—and what you are creating is gold as your dreams, and gold of your desires.

Now, that gold may be actual gold, for all we know, or it may be cash dollars or pounds or euros or something else equally valuable in its own way.

It may be qualities of experiences; it may be types of relationships; it may be just more delicious ideas.

It doesn't really matter.

Your ability to create is only limited by your imagination; and we know that from where you sit there is an infinite number of ideas at your fingertips.

All you need do is turn your attention to what is bigger and broader and more expanded from where you are, and you will find all manner of delicious ideas waiting there to be discovered.

And as you do so—as you see yourself there in the picture, having what you're wanting—as you feel yourself in alignment with what you know is coming—the way to get there will immediately present itself.

The only delay will happen because you are not quite sure you can have what you're wanting.

And so, our invitation for you today is to start loosening that up a little bit.

Start dreaming a little bit bigger; start imagining a little bit more than what you've imagined before, and see if you can find a way to demonstrate for yourself that you can indeed have exactly what it is that you are wanting; and that what you are wanting—there is no limitation to this very, very delicious, very wonderful series of creations that are coming through you again and again.

6. The next step on your journey is always the step that feels better from where you are

The next step on your journey—and this is something that we would suggest applies to any topic whatsoever—the next step on your journey is always the step that feels better from where you are.

And what we mean by this is that your intuition is always guiding you—always guiding you—on how to get from where you are to where you want to be.

What you will notice that is different between taking the path of intuition as opposed to the path of logic, is that things are not laid down in a straight line for you necessarily when you are following your intuition.

Rather, using what we might call the "Law of Efficiency," you are guided each step of the way—not because there is some unseen hand moving you—but because, as you're moving forward creating your reality, creating whatever it is that you are summoning to you, allowing those things to come into your experience—as you're following that path—the thought that feels better, the words that feel better in their speaking, and the action that feels better in its doing right at the moment as you do it, right at the moment as you say the words, right at the moment that you think the thoughts—as you follow this, what happens is you are led to the very next best place, considering the totality of all that you are creating.

So, when you are spinning straw into gold—when you are creating money as opposed to making money—what you will discover as you practice this more and more, and become more adept at it and more accustomed to it, is that the agenda that you think you're bringing to your experience may not necessarily be the one that is exactly what you really want.

It may just be the one that you think, "I need to get this done now."

And if you examine why you are thinking that, you will probably discover that the reason why you are thinking, "I need to get this done now," has something to do with what you think you should be doing, or what someone else thinks you should be doing, or what you believe they think you should be doing.

But it's not really plugged in or connected to or tuned into your Source.

It's rather just your—and we mean this in the most loving way—arbitrary idea that, "This is the next thing that I'm supposed to do."

When you're following the thought that feels better, when you're following the action and the words that feel better, what happens is that a plan, so to speak, begins to emerge from within you that's actually much more brilliant and much more connected to and much more tuned into who you really are than what you may be accustomed to thinking about otherwise.

Now, we're not saying that you're not brilliant, because you all are amazingly brilliant and very plugged in to who you are.

It's just that you've been taught to figure things out —and the problem is, you're figuring things out as if you have limited data upon which to make decisions.

So, if you follow what feels better—if you follow your intuition, if you follow that next step that feels better in its doing—not because it will bring you something later, but because you know right now that it just feels better, two wonderful things happen.

One is that you go in the direction of exactly where you're really wanting to go. And it's not just that you're going in that direction to eventually arrive there; you are literally in that moment becoming more and more and more of what you have been dreaming into being.

So, in other words, that's literally how the straw becomes gold.

Each of those moments become golden as you follow your intuition.

So, as you go in that direction and as you follow your intuition in this way, not only do things begin to unfold in this very, very delicious way, what also begins to happen is you begin to drop the resistance that you have to who you are wanting to become.

The way you can tell you have this resistance is because you are not there yet.

Now, your job is not to search out the resistance and obliterate it and kill it or destroy it—at least from our perspective.

What we're noticing is that the simplest, most efficient, most direct way to get to where you want to go is literally to follow your intuition, because then you will be moving into those moments where dropping resistance becomes a natural, easy, normal, simple thing to do.

So, as you are spinning straw into gold, you are literally finding the gold coming from the straw.

In other words, there's these wonderful moments that are golden—that are just delicious—where not only do you feel the powerful, tremendous abundance that you are creating for yourself—not only is that happening—but also within you there is emerging a knowingness, a certainty, a clarity about who you are, and you are becoming increasingly more confident in your ability to make a decision about what you will have, and then let what you will have show you the next step and the next step through your intuition.

Because remember: when you are thinking of something—when you are imagining something—you are giving birth to an idea; and that idea, in essence, has its own directions.

It comes with its own path and pattern; and you can't have a question—as we've said before—that does not have an answer.

You can't have a goal that does not have a way to get there.

Everything that you can imagine and everything that you can conceive of, you can achieve, you can create, you can experience.

And as you follow what feels better, you build more and more trust in your own innate inner knowing that transcends the small ways that you trained yourself and have been trained to look at the world around you.

Sometimes this is going to feel like stepping out on trust or on faith; but if you literally are following what feels better, it's just going to be the obvious next thing.

And yes, other people may look at you and say, "Wow, you're really trusting; you have a lot of faith."

And you might say—will probably say, actually—"It doesn't feel like trust or faith to me; it just feels like the next obvious thing," because you are following your intuition, and you've built a continuously strengthening and grounded foundation from which to continuously move forward into more and more of what you are creating.

The thing that is the most perplexing (we're noticing from most of our physical friends when we talk about this) is how this is actually very simple and there's no complexity to it whatsoever.

The thing that is confusing, we notice, is that instead of doing X so that you can get Y—in other words, instead of doing this so that you can get to that—following your intuition is actually all about: "What is the next this?"

You're not trying to figure out How will this help me? or How will this support me? or How will this ground me? or How will this move me forward?

Instead, what you're realizing is that when you follow what feels better—the thought that feels better, the words that feel better in speaking, the actions that feel better in their execution—what you're doing is your vibration is expanding, because you're literally following what feels better.

And as you feel better and better, and your vibration expands, you will understand that everything is vibration.

And in this forward movement, what happens is that you have the ability in each moment to feel a little bit better and a little bit better, until you begin to realize—after not a very long period of time, in fact, if you're somewhat persistent about this—that you've really moved quite a way from where you were, and now you are becoming the very thing that you were dreaming of.

The reason why you're spinning straw into gold is because of what you believe the gold will bring you: more freedom, more joy, more happiness, more contentment, more satisfaction.

All of which is fine.

The wonderful thing is, you don't have to wait for circumstances to change; and, in fact, when you become aligned with that vibration—the vibration of freedom, the vibration of abundance, the vibration of joy, of happiness, of satisfaction—when you become aligned with those vibrations, what happens is quite simply you become the thing that you are creating.

And so, physical reality will shift—as it does all the time—will shift around to match the vibration that you are asserting.

So, today we invite you to test this, to try it out.

"What is the thought that feels better?"

Ask yourself this question.

And notice that we're saying better and not good—something that we like to remind our physical friends of quite a bit.

Sometimes the thought that feels better does not feel good, depending upon where you feel vibrationally.

But if you just keep asking yourself, "What is the thought that feels better? As I'm speaking these words, do I feel better as I'm speaking them?" and be willing—or at least give it a try—that if, as you are speaking, you can feel your energy going down, that you stop speaking until you find a word that feels better to speak.

And if you are taking an action and you find your energy going down—you find that you're getting tired; you find that you're withdrawing from yourself—to stop what you're doing until you can find the next action that actually does feel better from there.

Play with this, test it out; see what happens.

But we do invite you to follow your intuition in this way, and to see all of the really delicious experiences that can come forth as a result of doing so.

You've been dreaming tremendously wonderful things into being, and they are coming—and following what feels better is your fastest way to get to where you want to go and to be there with them vibrationally—and then watch the physical reality change to match the vibration that you're now asserting.

7. Appreciation amplifies anything that you are imagining

We have said before that imagination is the most powerful tool at your disposal.

When we say that, we don't mean imagination is something you should use as though it were this thing that was optional—that somehow you could get around in your life without imagining things.

What we mean is that imagination is something that you use all the time, and it is that most powerful tool that you have, and we'd recommend that you focus upon it.

We'd recommend that you begin to imagine more and more of what you are wanting; but one surefire way to amplify anything that you are imagining—particularly those things that you are imagining that you really want to experience, but are quite doubtful about whether or not you actually ever will—is to bring appreciation into the mix.

When you appreciate something in advance of experiencing it—when you find a way to fall in love with what it is that you are creating before it shows up—what you are literally doing is you are aligning yourself vibrationally with the very thing that you are wanting to have more of.

Now, culturally speaking, it's quite an interesting proposition to give thanks for that which has not yet been received, because it just doesn't make a lot of sense.

You don't have it yet; why would you give thanks for it?

And, in fact, in your culture the way you've been taught to deal with these things is to pout, or to push against, or to be upset that you don't have it—which makes a lot of sense: "I have a lack of something; I am upset with that."

But here, we're turning everything upside down and we're saying that when you realize that it's all about vibration, it's going to make a lot more sense to you to appreciate what you are creating long before you can actually see it, taste it, touch it, smell it.

When you give thanks in advance for that which you are creating, what you are doing is lining yourself up with what you would do in that moment when you actually do receive what it is that you are creating: you are going to have at least a brief moment of appreciation for what it is that you have brought forth.

So, when you amplify and magnify what you are imagining through appreciation—and you can feel in that heart-centered way how wonderful and delicious your experience that is yet to arrive is definitely already feeling—then you are lining up with the inevitability of the manifestation, and that's where all of this really happens.

We've said before: you do this all the time already; there's nothing new about anything that we're saying here.

What we're doing, in fact—perhaps—is we're just pointing out the obvious; but we're also helping you see how obvious it is.

There are lots and lots of things that you're in the habit of manifesting and creating out of thin air, but you don't think it's out of thin air; you think it's following some sort of logical path that you've done over and over again, when in fact what you're doing—when, for example, you create a peanut butter sandwich—is, you are imagining that you are having one, and then you're finding a way to line up with the having of it—which could be to assemble bread and peanut butter and a knife and bananas and honey and jelly or jam, or whatever it is that you like to have on your sandwich.

You are assembling these components together, and allowing a peanut butter sandwich to come through the inspired action that you take.

You don't think of it this way; you just think, "Well, I'm just going to make a sandwich."

But you have to know what a sandwich is before you can make it; and when you are appreciating the sandwich in advance of having it—and you can test this out for yourself today; you don't have to wait for anything else to happen—you can discover how appreciation amplifies the experience: when you appreciate the sandwich in advance of its creation, it's a lot tastier when it arrives, and you're clearer about what you really want.

So, if you're in the habit of just making a sandwich to make a sandwich and you're thinking, "Oh, I'll just make a sandwich and I'll have my lunch, or I'll have my dinner, or I'll have my meal or snack" (or whatever it is), and you're just making it to make it, well, that's fine and it does the job and it's okay; it's no big shakes.

But when you take a moment to appreciate the sandwich before it arrives, that allows you to do several different things:

One is, it allows you to refine and define your experience, because what are you giving thanks for?

"Well, I'm giving thanks for sustenance," you might say, or "I'm giving thanks for the nutrition," or "I'm giving thanks for the taste or the texture or the quality of the experience."

And, again, these might seem like very silly, simple things; but when you take these and practice them on something as innocuous as a sandwich, and then apply it on much bigger things—things that you think are much more important than sandwiches, like money, for example, or experiences that you're drawing to you—as you're spinning your straw and you're thinking about how delicious it is to have what you're having now, and you bring appreciation into the mix—well, things really begin to take off, because you are lining yourself up not only with the experience that you know you'll be having, but you're also lining yourself up more importantly and more powerfully with your own Source Energy; because Source Energy sees all of your experience through the lens of appreciation.

Everything that you are, everything that you are becoming, everything that you are creating, everything that you are having—including all the things that you don't like, by the way—these are all seen through the lens of appreciation from that Source Energy perspective.

You have nothing but appreciation when you're plugged in and tuned in to Source Energy.

And when you're in that space, you're in the wanted aspect of everything; and we've talked about that before: how very, very useful and very powerful it is to be in your vortex—to be connected to your Inner Being, your Higher Self, to be plugged in to Source Energy in this way—because then all you see is the wanted aspect of everything that you are looking at; that becomes more and more of what you are experiencing, and things that come into your experience manifest along the lines of the wanted aspect.

There is no resistance, or there's a lot less resistance, and a lot more of what you are wanting gets through to you, because you are no longer saying, "I don't have it."

You're looking at it through the lens of appreciation, which means, "I have it."

You're looking at it through the aspect of the wanted end of things, which means, "I have it."

You're making yourself a vibrational match to the thing that you want, because you want to have it.

Well, when you begin to appreciate it, you are asserting the fact that you have it; the universe will and must and does respond to this.

So, your physical world rearranges itself according to these vibrations that you hold, and if the vibration that you're holding—particularly around what you are creating, what you're spinning into being—is appreciation, well, as you appreciate who you are becoming through the creation that you're creating, you're lining yourself up with all sorts of really, really good stuff.

And when we say good stuff, we mean all the really good stuff that is awaiting you in your vibrational warehouse—which is just the place that you store everything that it is that you've been dreaming of and imagining until such time as you become a match to that experience.

But all that's in your vibrational warehouse is the wanted aspect of things.

There's no unwanted anything in your vibrational warehouse.

So, in order for that to come to you, you have to line up with the wanted aspect of it.

Creating things in these deliberate ways—by applying the "Principle of Appreciation," we could call it—means simply that what you are doing is becoming the person that you are creating yourself to be, through the desire of the experiences and the things and the qualities of all of the different concepts that you are bringing forth into physical manifestation by your imagining; and your imagining is perfect and wonderful and delicious, and we invite you to do much, much more of it.

And we invite you, as you go through the day today, to notice if you can—and, if you will, appreciate—that which you are creating, even before it has arrived.

So, you could write a thank-you note to yourself for creating what it is that you have called forth, thinking about that place and time that is inevitably coming, where you will be thinking, "I'm really, really grateful and very much enjoying the fact that I created this experience. I'm here in the midst of it and I just love it."

You could write yourself a thank-you note; you could just sit down and enumerate the qualities of the experience that you are in love with—the experience that is to be had that is coming.

You could walk through your day noticing all of the things that you have created that you appreciate—now that you are a vibrational match to the having of them, and realize that this is going to be really the order of the day going forward if you want to tap into this power—and as you walk through the day and you're noticing, "Hey, this is really, really good stuff, the stuff that I've already manifested; that's what that feeling of appreciation feels like"; and you can apply that now to those things that you are creating that have yet to come into physical reality but are just waiting for you to line up with.

So, as you move through this powerful day of appreciation, and as you practice this principle and this art of appreciation, we know that what you're going to discover is how juicy it is to be in that space; and we suspect that you're going to want to be there more and more and more often, and we couldn't recommend that more highly.

It's a very powerful place to be; and when you couple appreciation with your imagination, and you give thanks for things that are wanted that have yet to arrive, you're really aligning yourself with the most efficient and expeditious way to have the very thing—the very thing—that you are wanting more of.

8. Your vibrational warehouse contains the wanted aspects of everything you are wanting

As we've said before, the task ahead of you is always to follow what feels better from where you are.

This is not something that you are required to do, and it's not something that we are insisting that you do.

It does mean that—if you follow what feels better from where you are—you will find yourself arriving moment after moment after moment into steadily improving conditions that are matching the totality of the desires that you are asserting, and that are existing already within your vibrational warehouse.

This vibrational warehouse of yours is quite vast; and stored within are all of the wanted aspects of everything that you have ever imagined or dreamed of —even in fleeting moments of thought—since the time you became who you are and who you identify yourself as now.

This vibrational warehouse is like a staging area, where all of the things that you are asking for and that you are imagining arrive instantly upon your imagining of them—or change shape immediately upon your re-imagining of them—and wait there until you become a vibrational match to what they are.

This warehouse is unlike any that you have ever seen in the physical plane: it is vast and immense and constantly growing.

If you were to experience everything that is in this vibrational warehouse, you would probably have to live about a thousand years; but even then, that wouldn't be long enough, because as you were experiencing all of these things you would be adding more to it.

When you croak—when you die—you will experience the wanted aspect of everything that is in this vibrational warehouse; so it is inevitable that you will experience everything that you are dreaming of; but we suggest that you not wait until you die to have what it is that you are wanting.

By lining up with the thoughts that feel better—following them where they go, speaking the words that feel better as you speak them, taking action only that feels better in its doing—you become more and more of a match to all of the things that you are wanting to experience that are now found in this vibrational warehouse.

You can easily imagine what this vibrational warehouse might look like: as you walk in its doors, what you would notice first is that everything that you see is in its most wanted aspect.

And you might be surprised that there are things that you notice that you don't remember wanting, but are there—and if you take a moment to think about them, you can remember, "Oh, this is where it came from; this is why I wanted it; this is what caused this experience—this object, this quality, this condition—to come forth into my vibrational reality."

As you walk through this vibrational warehouse and you look at what is there, you might see experiences played out like movies or tableaux or scenes on a stage.

You might notice that there is a vast room filled with all of the money that you have ever asked for and not yet lined up with.

And if you go through that room, what you'll notice is that the more you look at what is there, the more there is to see.

You could even imagine looking at—for example—a stack of currency notes, and as you watch them they become more.

It's as though the stack is getting larger and larger, higher and higher as you're watching it; because here in your vibrational warehouse you get to experience yourself as the powerful creator that you are, and you get to see how your creations come forth into your vibrational reality instantly.

You ask and it is given immediately—and you ask through your attention and your focus—and here you see it manifest right before your very eyes.

So, you can imagine going to someplace in this vibrational warehouse where it seems like there is a vast, empty room, and you could just begin to imagine all sorts of things that you might want, and watch them as they appear right before you.

And again, what you will notice is: what's in this vibrational warehouse is only the wanted aspect of things.

If you try to imagine something that you don't want, you'll notice that it changes right before your eyes into something you actually do want.

This vibrational warehouse—while not a physical place—represents pieces, parts, and ways in which you are assembling the physical reality that you are living in.

There is nothing here that you do not want; and the reason why, in your physical reality (your manifested reality) you experience things that you don't want is because of the resistance that you give them as they appear.

But there is no resistance in this vibrational reality, because here in this vibrational reality—this vibrational warehouse—here, this is the domain, if you will, of your Inner Being or your Higher Self.

This is just Source Energy in manifestation, manifested according to the ideas that you continuously assemble as you're going through your life, noticing what you have, what you don't have, what you want, what you don't want, and allowing the contrast of your experience to draw these things into your reality.

So, knowing about this vibrational warehouse and imagining its contents, and coming back from time to time whenever it pleases you to do so—whenever it feels better to do so—here, you can learn a lot about what it is that you are wanting.

Because if you bring something that is a mixed bag —that's a mixed vibration—into this vibrational warehouse, it will sort itself out right before your eyes.

It will reassemble itself into the wanted version, because there's no resistance here and resistance can't hold—it can't stand.

So that's why, when you're spinning straw into gold, what you're literally doing is you're taking withdrawals from the vast universal bank that is your vibrational warehouse.

You see: you've dreamed it; it exists already here, and now your job is to translate the experience into physical reality.

And the fastest, most deliberate, most efficient way to do this is to continuously follow the thoughts that feel better from where you are, the words that feel better in their speaking, the actions that feel better in their doing.

9. The actions that feel better in their doing

The next step on any journey is, of course, the next obvious step; and as you are learning to pay attention to your intuition and to follow the step that feels better—the thought that feels better in its thinking, the words that feel better in their speaking, the actions that feel better in their doing—as you are paying attention to these things and using them as the guides that they are, what you will find is that you are arriving at what you are wanting.

Today, we want to talk about the actions that feel better in their doing.

We know that there is a conversation extant in your culture about the importance of movement and doing and getting it done.

In a number of ways, you use motivational tools, you kick yourselves, you try to shame yourselves into taking action; and we would suggest that this has never really worked as it was intended to do.

In other words, you can try really hard, and you can probably actually succeed after expending a great amount of effort by doing these things on your own and by yourself, without any of the inborn assistance that comes with you.

But what we want you to understand is that it's no longer necessary, if you don't want to do that anymore.

We would suggest that you follow your own internal guidance, which is always leading you to exactly what it is that you are wanting.

When you do this, what you will notice is that there is a greater efficiency in your life: that things get done more quickly; that what you are really wanting actually rises to the surface very, very fast; and that it's not anything that is needed to be done, but you find yourself doing lots and lots of things that you want to do.

So, as you follow the actions that feel better in their doing, one of the things that you will learn over time is how to discern the difference between what you were taught—which is, "I'm doing this in order to get something later," which may be twenty seconds later, a minute later, a day later, a year later—and "I'm doing this because right now, right here, right in this moment, this feels like something very delicious to me; this feels better to me in the doing of it."

As you learn how to discern this, and as you become more and more adept at it, you will probably become quite amazed at what you are able to accomplish with very little effort.

Because if you are always following the action that feels better—or mostly following the action that feels better—and doing only that—or mostly that—what you will discover very quickly is that there's not an awful lot to do, because each of your actions is the most efficient and is the one that gets you there quicker.

Now, sometimes you're not going to know that ahead of time; and that's another very interesting, new thing that you will learn and that you will discover for yourself.

As you practice this over time, you will develop trust and confidence in your ability to create what you are wanting by simply following the actions that feel better in their doing; but there will be times when you will take an action and you will not know exactly why you're doing it or what it's for—and that's perfectly fine, because sometimes it is useful—as you will see with confidence and with clarity as you do this time and time again—sometimes it is useful to go in one direction and then to make a turn and go in another direction.

So, as you practice this, you will also learn to let go of what we might very lovingly call your addiction to consistency.

What we notice from our physical friends is that your teachers and your parents—very well-meaning individuals—try to make it very, very clear to you that it's important to not only do good but to look good while doing it.

And what we mean by this is that you don't want

anybody to think you're kind of crazy by being inconsistent in your behavior.

You want your behavior to be pretty obvious around you, so that in case you are called on it—like a pupil trying to prove his or her work during a math test —you have the ability to say, "No, this is the reason why I'm doing this: because it's what is logical and this is what anyone else would do."

So many of the internal conflicts that you bring to us in our conversations with you really stem from this dilemma: "There's this thing that I want to do, but it conflicts with the thing that I'm supposed to do"; and the thing that you're supposed to do generally arises not out of any really clear logic, but actually out of a sense of obligation to appear consistent and logical in your behavior.

When you are following the action that feels better in its doing, and you are taking those actions, what you will discover is that the benefit of feeling better actually outweighs your need for consistency.

What you will discover is that just taking an action that feels better in its own right is, in a way, its own reward, because you feel better and you're building a momentum of downstream movement where things get better and better progressively as you are feeling better and better.

So, as you're going out through your day today, we recommend that you think about: "Am I doing what I'm doing because of what will happen later, or am I doing what I'm doing because of what I'm feeling right now?"

And as you discern the answer to that question—over and over again—you will probably notice the places where you really do follow what feels better right in the moment, because it's just a habit that you have cultivated, particularly around specific topics or on specific issues.

But the issues that are thorny in your life—the ones that give you pause, that you are concerned about—particularly things perhaps having to do with money, or the use of money, the spending of money, the saving of money, the making of money—around these topics—and not just them—but around these topics you might be surprised to see how much strategizing you're doing, trying to figure out, "Now, if I do this, will it provide the result that I want later?"

When you do this, what you are doing—and, again, for very well-meaning reasons—is you are abandoning the internal guidance that you came with.

Now, to be fair, everyone that you know was taught to do this by people who thought it was the very, very best way to get through a chaotic experience in a chaotic universe.

But if you really do pay attention to your internal guidance, you will notice that you always know what is the action that feels better to you from where you are.

And, again, we want to make the strong distinction between actions that feel better because of what will happen later—"I'll do this now so that I can feel better later; I'll eat these peas so that I can have some ice cream afterwards"—there is a distinction between this

71

and following what feels better right now—noticing that, as you are reaching for the telephone or putting finger to keyboard or just literally walking across the room, that that action actually feels better in its execution.

And no matter where you are or what you're doing —no matter what the topic may be, no matter what the situation may be—there always is an action that feels better than any of the others, and there's always an action that feels better in its doing that's obvious if you just pay attention to it.

Remember that you've got many, many years of experience doing things for a delayed result.

So, it may take a little bit of time and a little bit of effort to learn how to do things because they feel better right in the moment.

Now, we want to make one thing very clear: When we talk about feeling better, we're not talking necessarily about a physical feeling—although that may be exactly how it manifests itself.

What we are talking about is an improved vibrational state, where you just feel a little bit better from where you were before.

This is primarily an emotional state, but it may very well manifest itself physically.

So our suggestion to follow what feels better right now is not really a call to hedonism—although perhaps that is what you are called to—but rather is a call to staying very aware of where you are in the present moment.

Now, you're not going to do this perfectly; in fact, you may not do it very well at all, but any small improvement in this area will actually yield tremendous rewards.

First of all, you're just going to feel better—and that, in and of itself, is quite wonderful; expanding vibrational states are always a very, very good thing, because everything is vibration.

But, not only will you feel better, but you will see the results working themselves out through you in very practical, grounded, physically-orientated ways, which will increase your confidence in your ability to pay attention to your own inner guidance; and that, we think, is a very, very good thing indeed.

So, we do invite you today to go through your day asking yourself the question, "Am I doing what I'm doing because of what I think it will bring me later, or am I doing what I'm doing because it feels better to me right now?"

And as you continue to go through the day discerning the answer to that question, we think you will be very pleasantly surprised at how many times you actually are doing what you're doing because it feels better to you in the moment; and in those instances where you are obviously, clearly doing what you are doing for some future reward, or future yield, we think you will notice very quickly that there are other alternative; and, perhaps even better, it will begin to dawn upon you that suffering and sacrifice are not needed in order to have everything that you are creating in your life.

10. Stopping to smell the roses along the way

The end of any journey is never really clear as you're walking along the path, and this is true for two reasons:

First, because the end of the journey changes as you are walking along the path.

The path itself actually is very much part of the unfolding of the journey—and we don't mean just that you put one foot in front of another—but rather, each moment as it unfolds brings something new to the experience, and so by the time you arrive at where it is that you intended to go, your very destination has changed because of the journey that you took.

The other reason why it's never really about the destination and it's always about the journey is because you never actually really do get there.

Whenever you do "arrive" at some place or some

75

destination—having achieved some goal or having received something that you asked for—simultaneous to this, if not antecedent to it, there is a new launching of desires that is entwined with what it is that you are creating, that then almost seemingly magically pushes everything forward.

Now, we don't mean that you're on a treadmill—an endless loop—or that the journey itself is so important at the very small level that that's really all you should pay attention to.

It's delicious to have the goal of the journey, whatever it may be: in this particular context we might say to create the money, to create the situation that is abundant and overflowing.

But when you realize that it really is all about the journey—because of what the journey does to the destination, and how the destination is constantly in flux because of where your journey goes, and how all of your power is right here, right now in the present moment—then you know that wherever you are in your journey, this is where your power is.

It's not ever going to be when you get there.

It's always going to be right here, right now, wherever that may be, whenever that may be.

So, if you are doing what you are doing because you want to get somewhere else, and this moment—this action, this thought, these words—are just expediencies to get you from here to there, we invite you to rethink that and to bring more of your attention back to really what does feel better from right here, right now.

Whenever you're tangled up in the goal of where you're going—and you're focused upon it in that way that distracts you from where you are, and you're thinking only about the thing that you need to do or the thing that needs to happen or the thing that needs to come to you—first of all, you're missing a whole lot of really good stuff that's going on around you.

Now, all of this may sound very trite, because it can be reduced down to some rather silly sayings, like "Stop and smell the roses," which is of course a very good idea, but it's so silly because it is so trite, so often said and so rarely applied.

But if you were to really stop and smell the roses, what would begin to happen is that your journey would become more rose-like.

Your experiences would become more in alignment with the sweetness of the smell of the roses, and you would find yourself more and more often in places where you really did want to stop and smell the roses— that actually would be your preferred action.

Now, as you train yourself in that direction—and by that direction we mean the direction of paying attention to where you are—as you train yourself vibration-ally more and more to that direction—finding the thought that feels better, looking for the words that feel better in their speaking, doing what feels better in its action, in its execution—what happens more and more often is that you become increasingly aware that wherever it is that you're going, that's inevitable.

So you might as well enjoy where you are, because

this is where everything is.

It's not going to be ten times better when you get to where you're going. It will be progressively better, because that's inevitable.

You're always undergoing expansion. You're always undergoing evolution. You're always opening up to more of who you are, even if you are actively resisting that.

But as you walk your path, as you get to where you want to go, what happens is—when you realize that the journey itself is where all the fun is, that this is where all the deliciousness is, this is where all the roses are, this is where it gets really, really good—then what you also begin to realize is that, because of the inevitability of the goal, the speed by which you arrive or the nature of your journey begins to become more of what is pleasing to you, more of what falls within the very delicious preferences that you have established; and it is less and less about what you should be doing.

And when you are doing what you "should" be doing—any time you are doing that, any time you are taking an outside preference, any time you are doing something because of what you think you should be doing, or how it will happen later, or how you'll maybe get there at some point, and this is what you're going to do right now in order to make that happen—any time you're doing any of that, you're missing what is actually right under your very feet, which is always really, really amazing.

So, we invite you today to stop and smell the roses,

to pay attention to what's happening around you, to use your physical senses as a really wonderful, delicious way of grounding into the present moment.

Listen for the sounds that are pleasing, and hone in on them; smell into the aromas that are stimulating and wondrous; look for the things that are beautiful, the colors, the textures, the ways that things are arranged.

Look for the sunrise, look for the sunset; look for the sun in the sky or the clouds passing by.

Look at who is around you, and look at how amazing they are and how beautiful they are.

Feel, run your finger over the surface of whatever is around you and feel what it feels like. Is it cool? Is it warm? Is it pebbly? Is it soft? Is it smooth? Be where you are.

Now, we know you're not going to do this perfectly, by any stretch, but the more that you can pay attention to what's going on right here, right now, and the more that you find ways to appreciate it, the more you're going to realize that you are already where it is that you want to go—that there really is no delay in having what you are wanting.

So, we invite you to go through the day today experimenting with this—playing with it—realizing that this literally is how you spin straw into gold.

It's your awareness that the straw is gold—that the basic components of what you are wanting are actually already assembled into the very thing that you want.

It's a matter of you training your perception in that direction; and by practicing—noticing where you are, what's going on, what it smells like, what it looks like, what it tastes like, what it feels like, noticing right where you are right in the moment, two or three or four or ten or as many times today as you can remember to do so—you will be plugging into exactly where the gold is.

It's right here, right now.

Now, at first it's not going to seem as though there's a practical application here; in other words, if you're asking the question, "Where's my money?" and we're saying, "Look, stop and smell the roses," we don't mean that there's a stack of money underneath the rosebush.

But what we do mean is that by training your attention to go in that direction and to be present where you are, you become alert and attentive to all of the ways that your inner guidance is showing you, "Go in this direction; this is where it is: this is what will bring you more and more of what you're wanting."

But more than just training your attention in that direction, paying attention to where you are—stopping to smell the roses—will be, by its very definition, very, very sweet.

And, we can only imagine that after a little bit of doing this, you will find it to be an immensely pleasurable and delicious experience.

11. There will never be enough time or money in the world to satisfy the need for time and money

There will never be enough time or enough money in the world to satisfy the need for time and money.

And what we mean by this is that as long as you see any one thing or any set of things as being in short supply, and what you are wanting is to have more of it so that you don't have less of it, you will find yourself in a constantly spinning circle of trying harder and harder to get more and more of what it is that you are vibrationally declaring you do not have enough of.

Now, the universe will deliver to you anything that you're asking for, but it brings you the totality of what you are asking for; and so, if what you are doing is vibrationally saying, "I must have this because I do not have it," then, while you may receive it, the feeling of incompleteness will surround the having experience of it.

So, what we invite you to do today is to spend some time, as you're going through your day, looking for evidence of what you have already; and affirm the having of it from a place of abundance and expansion.

In very practical terms, the way this might look is that you might turn to, for example, your bank account; and regardless how much money there is or is not in the bank account, you might see if you can spend a little bit of time noticing that it's wonderful to have what you have, even though it might not be what you want right now at this moment.

There's nothing wrong with it. In fact, it's a very good thing indeed to want more than what you have, because that is how the expansion of all things happens.

However, there is a very big difference—and perhaps today you will find the difference vibrationally—between, "I don't have it and I need it," and "I don't have it and I want more of it."

Because when you're saying, "I don't have it and I want more of it," what will happen is—over time—you will become more and more accustomed to the having of it through the desires that you're launching; and you will no longer say, "I do not have it"; what you will begin to say—and we invite you to go start this journey today, if you have not started it already—is you will begin to say, "Everything that I have is wonderful, and I

82

want more from where I am."

There is indeed no lack in the universe; there is no end to what you can create; there is no finite quantity of anything.

Your universe—your physical universe—is a perfect vibrational match to your assertion; and if you are noticing lack, you will experience lack.

If you are noticing fear, you will experience fear.

If you are noticing that things are not going right, things will not go right; because in your assertion you are always correct.

So, today we invite you to change your mind; and perhaps this is the continuation of a long-ago-started journey, but we do invite you today to remember that this is where it all begins—because today is a new beginning—and to change your mind about the having state of your experience: to begin to affirm that you have; and that although you have, you do want more; and that while you have, you do want more; and given that you have, you do want more; and delicious because you have, you do want more; because you're enjoying the having of it, you do want more.

Because it's so delicious to have what you're having that you're wanting more and more of it; and as good as it gets right now with the having of it—which is really delicious—you're wanting more and more of it from where you're sitting.

So, if you go back and look at these words again, what we have just said was a gentle vibrational expansion into a more and more open space where the affirm-ation of the perfection of where you are becomes the primary thought that then launches you into expansion of more and more.

Again, in very practical terms this might look like sitting and looking at a bank balance—or the contents of a wallet—until you are able to appreciate what you are having right now, and feel the freedom and the joy— even if it's just for a moment—of what that having feels like.

It might help you to remember that you are the one who created what you are having, and this delicious creation is of your own doing; and what you have created is always worthy of honor—not because you must get down on your hands and knees and hope and pray that the having that you have right now will be helpful in the future, or that somehow it will turn out to be better than it is right now—but because, literally, in this moment, what you have created is exactly right for you.

And when you notice this from a place of appreciation—which may take a little bit of effort from where you are—but when you notice this from appreciation, you will feel the surge of joy and freedom that happens when you liberate your creations from the role that you have given them.

Because today, what you will be noticing is how you have made your creations into the jailor of your experience:

You have assigned them the role of reminding you of lack.

And today—if only for a moment—you will be, as

you practice this thought, opening up to the possibility of abundance coming from where you are, not in spite of where you are.

Another way to think of this is to remember that you are a progressively expanding being of light.

Your training thus far, culturally, has been to notice where things are not right, and to fix them. There is a logic to this that makes a lot of sense.

However, metaphysically, you are probably noticing that when you focus on what is broken with the intention of fixing it, the fix never really takes.

It might temporarily, but there's still something a little bit off.

And so, if you are making money in order to solve the "I don't have enough money" problem, even the money that you make will come to you in a way that feels incomplete.

Now, the wonderful thing is that it's never too late. Each moment is a new beginning, so you can always change your mind about what is happening in your experience.

But when you notice this, you will probably begin to notice that you have assigned the money that's coming to you the job of reminding you how you don't have enough money.

So, it might come to you tinged with a little bit of regret, or perhaps shame, or guilt, or even blame—perhaps even anger or fear.

And that's all right. You're not doing anything wrong here.

85

What you're doing is, however, something that you don't really want to be doing.

And so, by noticing that you are doing it, and turning your attention to what you do want to do instead—which is to appreciate what you are having, and allow that appreciation to launch you into the wanting and having of more of it—this is how literally you spin straw into gold: by appreciating the straw for what it is; appreciating the now moment for what it is, and how delicious it is, and how wonderful it is—and there's always a way to do that; while, at the same time, asking for more and more of what it is that you are wanting.

We know that as you go through this day today focused in this very delicious way, that possibilities that have long been present but not necessarily visible will present themselves to you; because now you're opening up to the having possibilities, the expansion possibilities.

Today is a turning point in this journey of spinning straw into gold.

Today is the day where you come face to face—if you so choose—with your creations; and you see the role that they have been playing for you, and how, just by appreciating them for what they are (no more complicated than that) you change their role, and they become something that supports you—honors you, just as you honor them—and reminds you that you are indeed a powerful creator, and that the abundance of the spheres is yours for the asking.

So, when you declare that you have plenty, and it's

wonderful and it's a perfect match, you are then free to become a match—most deliciously—to more and more of what it is that you are noticing.

We suggest that as you go through this day, that you find ways to bless what it is that you notice—that you find ways to appreciate them—for everything that you are seeing is of your own creation; and as you turn your attention to the wanted aspect of what it is that you have brought forth, you will find over and over again more and more of a joyful experience that resonates through and amplifies itself into more and more of your ever-expanding, ever-opening life unfolding.

12. Throughout the Universe there is a constant call to expansion

In the universe and throughout the universe, there is a constant call to expansion.

This call to expansion is happening through you right now, right where you are, no matter what you are doing, no matter what you are about.

There is within you a powerful, powerful desire to bring forth into physical manifestation ideas, concepts, desires, thoughts, passing fancies.

There is nothing noble or ignoble about ignoring your desires.

There is nothing right or wrong, good or bad, correct or incorrect about ignoring or not paying attention to what it is that you are wanting.

There is, however, a very strong and powerful call

that is the basis by which everything that you are wanting, and all of the strong desires that you do have, are being called forth into manifestation.

When you like something—when you are in alignment with it—what you are literally doing, as Source Energy in manifestation, is you are noticing the qualities and aspects of whatever it is that you like; and you are noticing those particular aspects and qualities in such a way as Source Energy would see them.

In other words, you're literally bringing the focus of All That Is to things that you probably consider to be very mundane.

The reason why we are speaking about this today is that we want you to begin to understand that your desire—quite specifically—to master the art of creating money and to spin straw into gold, is not arising out of nothing; it's not just a random thing, and it's also not produced by your reaction to things that happened in the past.

Your powerful desire to have more than what you have—to expand into more than what you are, to evolve into the broader version of the You that you are becoming—is literally the powerful call that creates all life everywhere.

You may think this is about money—and it certainly is, in this very specific instance—but in fact it's about the expansion of All That Is.

It may seem like that's too far of a stretch—that it's a little bit too much for us to be talking about it in this way—and if you are feeling that way, we invite you today to notice why it is that you consider money to be base or mundane, if you do.

You may be imagining that someone who really wants money is grasping—that they are greedy, that they are materialistic, that they are somehow or other not spiritual—and while those things may be the case with some individual people, the desire to have more than what you have is not materialistic, and it's not greedy and it's not grasping, in and of itself.

The desire to have more than what you have is literally the same desire that gives birth to whole new worlds.

It's the same desire that caused you to come forth into physical manifestation—that caused you to be born.

It's the same desire that animated your parents, and that animated you long before you knew you to be where you are.

This single, powerful desire is everywhere, and it's in everything.

The reason why a tree reaches towards the sun is because it wants to become more than what it is.

The reason why a flower blossoms and blooms is because it wants to become more than what it is.

The reason why a squirrel gathers nuts in the fall to prepare for the winter coming—in its own way, to store things away to have them later—is because the squirrel is wanting to become more than what it is.

The reason why anything is born is because it is wanting to become more than what it is.

The reason why—the true reason why—you are

wanting to spin straw into gold, and the reason why you are wanting to master the art of creating money, is because you are wanting to become more than who you identify yourself to be.

From where you sit right now, you may be thinking, "Well, this is actually what I'm really wanting—to be quite honest—is to solve this money problem that I have. I want the lack of money to go away and be replaced with the abundance of money. I want to feel rich; I want to feel wealthy."

And we're not saying that those things are not valid or worthy—although some of them are problematic metaphysically, because of their basis in lack.

But even that—even the most resistant reason why you are here in this conversation—even the most resistant reason is still based on the powerful desire for expansion: to become more than who you are.

Now, the key to understanding this very, very important idea is to realize that you are not becoming better from a place of worse—that you are not expanding into more graciousness from a place of baseness—that you are not expanding into a better place of abundance from a place of lack.

If you couch it in those terms, then you are missing the point.

The point is that where you are is perfect.

Where you are right now—no matter what your situation, no matter what your financial situation, no matter what your situation is in regard to money, no matter how much you understand or don't understand these words—where you are right now is perfect.

Nothing more is needed.

And you may think, "Well, that's just the opposite of what you just said"; but in fact, what we said is, "You want more."

We didn't say, "You need more."

You never need more; and if you will begin to understand that very simple idea—complex in application, we understand, but a very simple idea: that you don't need anything, but there is a whole heck of a lot that you are wanting—the more you understand this idea, the more you entertain this idea today—looking around to see, Is it right? Is it really true that you don't need anything? Is it really true that all you're really wanting is to just become more of who you are?—as you think about these things—as you contemplate them—we invite you to notice that even the worst situation that you might be in actually has its own inner perfection.

And so you don't need to leave that situation; but we certainly understand that you might have a very powerful desire to want to leave it: to want to become more, to want to expand into something that is broader, more open, more inclusive, more abundant, more prosperous, more filled with the money experience in all of its wanted aspects.

For, you see, when you understand these things, even just a little bit—even if you just have a glimpse into this—what you will notice is—what we are saying here is that as you line yourself up with wanted aspects, what you are wanting will come forth into manifestation.

We've talked about this idea in a series of different ways throughout this conversation.

Wanted aspects lead to wanted experiences.

Noticing those aspects leads to experiencing those aspects.

If you line yourself up with what is wanted, you will have what is wanted.

This is just simply how Law of Attraction, that single organizing principle, works in action.

So, as you go out through the day today, we suggest and we invite you to notice: Do you really need anything?

Find out the answer to that question, and see if what's really going on is that there are a whole lot of things that you are wanting; and that in the wanting of those things, the very universe itself—All That Is, Source Energy—is expanding itself through you.

It will only take a moment of awareness about that for you to feel the magnificence of this idea, and to realize that the most mundane things that are happening in your life, where you're wanting something more from where you are, are worthy of great honor, because they are literally the ways in which Source Energy expands into more of what it is becoming; and that is always a very good thing indeed.

13. There is within you a very strong desire to have everything you are wanting

There is within you a very strong desire to have what it is that you are wanting.

In your lifetime, you may have been trained—or trained yourself—to disregard this desire; and you could have done so for several different reasons.

For instance, you might have decided that since you're probably not going to get what you really want, you might as well not really want it; or you might have decided that since it's probably not appropriate for you to have what you really want, you shouldn't want it; or you don't want to be greedy, or you don't want to be grasping, or you don't want to reach for something that really could harm other people if you have it.

All of these thoughts—all of these ideas—are based

upon the false premise that, somehow or another, you having what it is that you're wanting can either take something away from someone else or harm them or yourself.

And we do like to say that that is a false premise, because when you are having what you are really wanting, the exact opposite is true.

When you are having what you are really wanting, you are affirming the abundance of All That Is.

When you are having what you are really wanting, it is a powerful invitation to the people in your life—to the people around you—to have what they really want.

Now, you might notice that what we're saying here is *having what you're really wanting.*

What we mean by this is, there are these powerful desires that rise up within you as a result of the contrast that you experience in your life.

These are the things that you really want.

If you are accustomed to sorting things out according to what is appropriate and what isn't, this might be very difficult to discern; but as you are learning how to pay more and more attention to what feels better to you right from where you are—in other words, as you're learning how to pay attention to your Inner Being speaking to you, that internal guidance that is always there, rising up naturally in each moment—as you become more accustomed to paying attention to that inner signal, it will become obvious what it is that you really want.

You may be accustomed to organizing your physical reality—again—according to what is appropriate and what you should and should not do and what you should and should not have.

When you are doing this, what you are doing, essentially—from a vibrational perspective—is you are reinforcing lots and lots of things that you know you really don't want.

For instance, you are reinforcing that there is a chaotic universe out there that all of your rules and all of your internal needs, as you've defined them, are protecting you from.

And Law of Attraction, being what it is—the single organizing principle of the universe—will bring you evidence of how you are correct.

But, as you turn your attention to the realization that you are living in an already perfectly organized experience, and that Law of Attraction has been organizing it for you according to where you've been putting your attention—including to the things that you don't like—then you are beginning to get the idea that you can have what it is that you really want, and that it will not hurt you or anyone else—that it does not take anything away from anyone else, nor does it deprive you of anything.

No sacrifice is required; no hurt must be endured; no pain must be suffered through.

It's simply this: you become a vibrational match to the wanted aspects of all of that that you have been amassing in your amazing vibrational warehouse.

It's all there: all of the really good stuff that you've

been asking for since the very beginning of you.

And when you let go of this false premise that having what you really want is painful or hurtful or means lack in some way, you will discover that so many of these things—experiences, situations that you have been asking for, particularly in the realm of money—have been right at your fingertips all along.

They've never really been outside of arms length; they've always been right there.

You've just been very busy ignoring them and trying to pretend as though they did not exist.

If you will approach all of this with as much compassion and kindness for yourself and for other people as you can muster, you will find it very easy to relax into the inevitability of the powerful desires that you've been launching.

And so, today as you're going throughout your day, we invite you to look at your manifested physical reality with as much compassion, kindness and gentleness as you can: to bring a very soft lens, a very open stance, and a very relaxed approach to how you navigate your physical experience.

There is always within you the ability to see the perfection of all that you have created up to this point, and we invite you to look for that perfection with great compassion, with great kindness, and with great gentleness towards yourself and all of the other people who have been involved in these creations.

We know that you will find things that you don't like; but if you can look at those things with compassion and kindness, what we think you will notice is that you really did do the very best you could, considering what you knew and who you were and who you were becoming at that moment.

There really is nothing wrong with what you are experiencing; but there are many things about it that you may not like.

So, as you are making peace with all of the ways in which you have been keeping what you really want at bay and suffering through what you thought you should have, we know that what will happen is you will begin to turn your attention back again and again to what you really do want; and as you're spinning straw into gold today, what you will discover is that all of the reasons why you want the g

old—everything that has led you to this moment of powerful, strong desire—is exactly right.

There's nothing wrong with these powerful desires.

And, as you look at them from the wanted aspect of everything, it will be easier and easier and for you to allow that great spinning wheel to bring forth into manifestation these very delicious, wanted, physical aspects.

So, as you're going through your day today, being very kind and very gentle and very compassionate with yourself and with all of the other people who have been part of the story so far, you're setting the ground— you're setting the stage, you're preparing the way—for more and more of this very, very allowing, very open, and very aligned approach to having what it is that you are really wanting.

And you will see quite quickly, we believe, how exactly right that is, and how perfectly everything has brought you to this moment, and why it could not and should not have been any different than it was.

And this is always a very good thing.

14. Thinking a thought that feels better from where you are

The next step on any journey is always the thought that feels better from where you are.

You've heard us say this several times now, and we come back to this topic again and again, because this really is the answer to just about any question that you can bring forth about what is next, or what to do, or where to go, or who to talk to in terms of creating more and more of the money that you're wanting in your experience.

So, if you will take a moment as you're going through the day today and think about what it is that you're wanting—bring that into focus; think about how it feels; feel your way into it—notice what arises as you're feeling, because you will begin to see contracting

101

thoughts that arise if there is a thought within you that contradicts the desire that you have.

Pay attention to these things, and find the thought that feels better from where you are.

So, today we want to talk in more depth about what it means to follow the thought that feels better.

Previously we spoke about following actions that feel better in their doing, and today we want to talk about those thoughts that feel better.

On the one hand, this is a pretty simple topic.

You think thoughts; some thoughts feel worse, some thoughts feel better.

Perhaps you might think that thoughts come to you randomly, as though you were being assailed by them—or as though you were sailing a ship through uncharted waters and you occasionally come across things that you've never seen before, some of which are helpful to you and some of which are not.

No matter how you approach this, we want to remind you that you are the thinker of your thoughts; they do not arise out of nothing.

Every thought that you think is an idea that is expressing itself through you, because of you, caused by you.

So, as you go through your day today, it might be very helpful indeed to just pay attention to the thoughts that you are thinking and to discern, "Does this thought feel better as I'm thinking it, or does it feel worse as I'm thinking it?"

Now, if it is helpful, you can assign a value to the

thought that you are thinking, and decide, "Well, this thought feels like joy; and this thought feels like hopefulness; and this thought feels like contentment; while this thought feels like boredom; this thought feels like frustration or irritation; this thought feels like jealousy; this thought feels like revenge; this thought feels like fear or despair."

But regardless of how you name the thought and the feeling that arises—which is just the vibrational resonance that the thought creates—however you name that feeling—that vibration—it really comes down to something very basic:

A thought that feels better is going in the direction of all that you are creating; that is why it does feel better.

It resonates—this thought—with the totality of who you are.

You could think of it as your Inner Being—your Higher Self—calling you forth.

When you think a thought that feels better, that's your Inner Being telling you that thought is more in alignment with who you are than where you were before, so it's an improvement.

When you think a thought that does not feel better —that feels worse—that's your Inner Being saying to you, "This thought is not in alignment with who you are, and in fact has moved you further away from that alignment."

Now, let us be clear: Your Inner Being is not standing there with a chalkboard or with a clipboard keeping score or taking note of how well you're doing.

All that's happening is that, in each moment, you're getting instantaneous feedback from that internal guidance system that says whether or not what you are thinking is more in alignment with who you are or not.

When you understand why this alignment is so important, it will be obvious why thinking a thought that feels better from where you are would be the only step you would ever take, at any time, regardless of what's going on.

This alignment that we speak of, with your Inner Being—with the totality of who you are, with Source Energy itself—this is important, because everything that you've been wanting—all of the things that you've been thinking of—can be found most easily and most readily from their most wanted aspect within that alignment.

So, another way of saying that is that as you follow these thoughts that feel better, it leads you into your vortex—and your vortex is just another way of describing that alignment.

When you get into your vortex—in other words, when you get into the vortex of that relationship that you have with Source Energy, with your Inner Being— there you are in the midst of all of the wanted aspects of everything that you have created through the thoughts that you've been thinking—through the powerful desires you have launched, through the contrast that you've experienced, on and on—but what is there is only the wanted aspect of things.

And so, you could say there is an efficiency to finding your way into your vortex—to finding your way into this alignment—because there you only have the wanted aspect of things.

So, then you don't have to deal with the messiness of the post-manifestational experience, wherein something that you've been wanting came forth into manifestation, but it came forth in a mixture of wanted and unwanted aspects, because at the point that you allowed it in, your vibration was in that mixed state.

There are many, many reasons why that would happen: primarily what we notice in your culture is that it happens because you're not quite sure you deserve to have what you're wanting; or you're not quite sure that what you are wanting is actually something that's worthy of being wanted; or you're not quite sure that you even really understand what it is that you're asking for, and so, in a way, you're taking it on faith that the thing that you want is something that you really do want.

But there's always that little question in the back of your mind: "Is this something I really want? Do I really need this? Should I want this?"—that sort of mixed vibration.

So, the more time that you spend in your vortex with the wanted aspects of everything, the more your manifestations—the experiences that you bring forth, the objects, the situations, the aspects of relationships—the more time you spend in your vortex, the more these manifestations come forth in their wanted aspect.

And then you build a forward momentum; you see?

And, in that forward momentum, what keeps happening is the more that you become a match to what you're really wanting, and your manifested ideas come forth in terms of objects or relationships or situations or experiences—the more that happens, the more you go in that direction just by default almost.

Because everything is going in that direction: in that direction of expansion, in that direction of more openness.

Now, let us be clear. Your vortex with your Inner Being—with your Source Energy, your Higher Self—is not a static place.

You don't just arrive there and everything is just very perfectly still and calm.

Now, it may be very peaceful—and certainly that aspect is definitely there if that's what you are wanting —but it's not devoid of movement.

Your vortex, in fact, is a highly dynamic experience where there is an almost accelerated path of evolution and expansion, because in your vortex you don't have a lot of resistance to who you are and who you are becoming.

So, all sorts of things are possible from there— things that were not possible before you got there, but that became increasingly possible as you continued to follow the thoughts that felt better.

So, following the thoughts that feel better today as you're going through your day—this is something that we do suggest.

We suggest that you experiment with what we are

talking about here, and see if you can notice the difference between a thought that feels better and a thought that feels worse.

Thoughts that feel better are going to have—to a certain extent—physical interpretations.

In other words, you might feel lighter; you might feel more open and more expansive; you might feel just more on track; you might feel more alive.

So, you're not just going to notice these feelings in your body; they are going to be experiences that you have—both physical and mental and emotional.

But you'll know, because you do know what feels better.

And thoughts that feel worse—you're going to feel the contraction of energy.

It might make you more sleepy; it might make you more irritated; it might make you angry.

But those are just vibrational states. In and of themselves, they're pretty insignificant.

They're just telling you, "Hey, this thought doesn't feel better. This thought feels worse; this thought is walking away, moving away from the truth of who you are."

So, as you play with this today and as you experiment with it today, we do suggest that you see how many thoughts you can think that feel better from where you are.

And a very important distinction here is to remember that these thoughts that feel better may not always feel good, right in that moment—but they do feel better from where you are.

And these thoughts are not designed to get you anywhere, because they are actually the movement in themselves.

So, you're not thinking a thought now—as we discussed previously with actions—you're not thinking a thought now in order to feel better later.

The thought that you are thinking now actually does feel better in its thinking.

You can feel the improvement; there's a tangible experience.

We've said this before in a slightly different way, but we do want you to remember that thinking thoughts that feel better from where you are—choosing those thoughts—in a way, is its own reward, because you feel better as you're thinking these thoughts; and as you feel better, then you want to think more of these thoughts, and the more that you think thoughts that feel better, the better you feel, on and on.

Again, it gains a momentum; you end up in your vortex and you end up feeling very connected—plugged in, tuned in—to who you are.

There is no thought that you can think that can truly really harm you or anyone else.

So, you're free to experiment with this and see, "Does this thought feel better? Does this thought feel worse?"

Remember that it is very simple and very basic.

It's like a red light or a green light. It's like a yes or a no. It's like an on or an off—very basic, very binary;

it's either the thought that feels better or the thought that feels worse.

And it's the thought that feels better that is the one that we invite you to find as many times as you can today—playing with this, being very easy with yourself and just noticing, "How does this work?"

15. Saying the words that feel better in their speaking

The next step on any journey is always the thought that feels better from where you are.

We've said this before, and today we want to bring your attention to—and invite you to think about—the words that feel better as you are speaking them.

We've discussed the actions that feel better in their doing, and the thoughts that feel better in their thinking, and today we want to talk about the words that feel better in their speaking.

So, as you're going through your day today, we invite you to notice whether what you are saying is bringing you more into alignment with who you are, or whether it is moving away from that place of connection.

Either way, you are either going to be becoming more of who you are or delaying that experience, but you cannot lose anything—and we really do want to bring that point home.

Any time you are disconnecting from yourself or pinching yourself off from Source Energy, all that is happening is that you are delaying the experience of your expansion; but it is still happening, even if you are not aware of it.

However, the most powerful place you can be—particularly in regards to money and spinning straw into gold—is to be constantly or consistently moving in alignment with yourself; and one very powerful way to be doing this, of course, is to be using the words that you are speaking, by only speaking those words that feel better from where you are.

Now, the way that you can tell whether or not you are doing this is, of course, by how you feel.

Because this entire conversation—none of it is about words, semantics, grammar, getting it right in any way, shape or form; it's all about the vibration— which is how you feel emotionally whenever you are speaking, whenever you are saying whatever it is that you are saying.

So, we invite you today, as you are talking—as you are moving around doing whatever it is that you are doing, and communicating whatever it is that you are communicating—we invite you to notice whether, when you speak, does your energy go up? Do you feel better?

Or does your energy go down, and do you feel worse?

And again, the important thing is not to try to get

it right; the important thing is to notice what it is that you are doing, and what it feels like when your energy is expanding as you are speaking, and what it feels like when your energy is contracting as you are speaking.

Again, when your energy is contracting, all that is happening is that you are delaying the experience of having what you are wanting.

When your energy is expanding, you are intentionally moving in the direction of what it is that you want more of.

Now, by default you're just as likely to be moving towards expansion as you are towards contraction.

If you're not paying attention at all, you can notice later on that you might feel better because of a conversation you had, but you don't really know why you feel better.

Or you might feel worse because of a conversation you had, but you don't really know why.

But when you are moving with intention and speaking words from that place of clarity and intention, what begins to happen is that you begin to feel better and better; and in that clarity—in that expanded place— you are tapping in, tuning in, plugging in to the Source of who you are—to your intuition, to that internal guidance system—and where you are going when you are doing this is to exactly where it is that you want to be.

You are literally in the process of creating your reality with intention, because your reality begins as a vibration first; and when your vibration is expanding, you know that you are becoming a match to all that it is that you have been wanting and asking for.

When your vibration is falling—when you're feeling worse—you're moving away from what you have been asking for.

You are delaying the experience of that expansion; you're delaying the experience of that place that feels better; you're delaying the experience of the manifestation of the wanted aspects of what you have been asking for.

So, as you go through the day today and as you pay attention to these things, we invite you to notice what feels better as you are speaking and what feels worse as you are speaking; and as you make this practice and as you become more and more adept at feeling the difference, we invite you to also go out a little bit more on a limb and venture to only say the words that feel better from where you are.

This might seem like a little bit of an adventure that has perhaps some peril attached to it, because what if the words that feel better are words that you don't want to say?

What we want you to understand is that the words that feel better in their speaking are going to have a maximally beneficial effect to everyone who is listening.

We don't know what that would be, specifically, and neither do you; but it is a powerful invitation when you are intentionally and actively connecting with the Source of All That Is—which is what is happening when you are speaking only the words that feel better from where you are; it is a powerful invitation to the people around you to do the same thing.

Some of them will experience you as a breath of fresh air, and some of them will experience you as being perhaps slightly irritating, because they may not be willing to go where it is that you're going; and that's quite fine and it really is none of your concern whether they go where you want them to go or not.

All that is your concern is to follow what feels better, because that's bringing you into alignment with You—capital Y-O-U—the part of you that is connected to All That Is.

And that, indeed, is always a very, very good thing; because as you are going down that path—which is really a journey without distance—what is happening is you are becoming the You that you have always wanted to become; you are drawing to you the experiences and all of their wanted aspects, and you are finding yourself more and more in exactly the right place at the right time, in the right way, with right people.

And when we say that, we don't mean that you are somehow orchestrating this; what we mean is that the inevitability of the perfection of what is already at play will become increasingly apparent, because as your vibration expands you will be able to see what Source Energy has already been seeing: which is that you are already in that perfect time, perfect place, with those perfect people, in that perfect way.

So, as you go through the day today experimenting with this—discovering what feels better as you are speaking—we also invite you to notice that there is no

115

formula here.

There is just how you feel.

Repeating the same words over and over again will not necessarily conjure up what it is that you are wanting.

As long as the words feel better to you, you know that you are in alignment; but you can say the same words again and again and find yourself moving out of alignment, and feel that contracting.

So, realize it's not the words; it's how you feel as you are speaking them.

And different words will mean different things at different times, based on where you are vibrationally; and you can immediately tell where things are going by how you feel as you are speaking.

So, as you're paying attention to this today, we think you're going to be quite delighted to notice how quickly—by finding words that feel better as you speak them—that you can shift your vibration into a place of greater and greater expansion, and feel continuously better and better, and find yourself in wonderful, wonderful experiences, and discover that—when you are spinning straw into gold—a key to this delicious, delicious experience is in what you say: not how you say it, but the vibrational experience of saying it.

And today you will understand that more clearly than ever before.

16. The only thing ever happening in your experience is creation

The only thing that is ever happening in your experience is creation.

What we mean by this is that you are not ever uncreating anything, and you are never going backwards in your experience.

You may feel from time to time, on the topic of money—particularly because it looks like money ebbs and flows; it looks like you have money one day and you don't the next—so you may from time to time think that somehow or another you got it right for a little while, but now you're not getting it right at all.

That would be a mistake, in our opinion, to draw that conclusion, and here is why:

The conclusion is based upon what your eyes can

see and what you measure in physical reality, and we want to remind you that physical reality is no gauge to where you are vibrationally.

Physical reality is the past; it's the manifested—already manifested—version of what it is that you are creating.

So, what we want you to understand is that when you look at your bank account or at your wallet and you say, "I'm not getting this right, because there's not enough money here," all you're doing is delaying an experience that is on its way; you're just making things a little bit slower and a little bit, perhaps, muddier and sludgier.

What we would recommend instead—particularly today—is that you find a way to look at what you see, and realize that what it's actually telling you is either nothing—in other words, look at the physical reality that you see and realize that whatever you're looking at is pretty meaningless—or give it the best positive meaning that you can find.

So, if you're looking at your wallet or your bank account and you're thinking, "There's not enough here; I must be doing something wrong," see if you can find a way to look at it instead and say, "The fact that it's empty means that more is coming"— which it does.

Each of you—everyone who is connected to what you are doing here—has more money in your vibrational escrow—in your vibrational warehouse—than you could possibly spend in a lifetime.

So, if you are temporarily "out of money" physically—or funds are low, or seem to be running low, or are going in that direction—it's perfectly correct, from a vibrational perspective, to assert that more is coming; because when you assert that more is coming, what you are doing is lining up with an idea; and Law of Attraction, being what it is, will come around and make you right—bring you evidence of how correct you are.

When you assert that you are wealthy—that more money is coming, that this is temporary and it's going to get better—you're always correct.

So, today we invite you to be mindful of what you are seeing, and remember that what you are seeing does not show you that you're not doing it right.

What it is showing you is what the potential is.

Now, for some of you—as we said earlier—it may be better—it may be easier—to start off by saying, "Well, I don't really know what any of this means. I don't know what it means that I don't have money in my bank account or in my wallet, or that there's not enough, or that I want there to be more and there isn't. I really don't know what that means."

That may be a simpler way to start off things.

The point here is to make peace with what you are seeing, and to turn in the direction of what you want more of.

We don't suggest that you do this with great effort or with a lot of pushing.

What we suggest is that you ease your way into it; find the thought that is easiest to get to.

But, ultimately, we do suggest that you find the

119

most positive interpretation that you can give to whatever it is that you are looking at.

As we said at the beginning: it's never possible to uncreate or to badly create.

Once something is created, it's done.

We know that what happens often for our physical friends is that there are things that you have created that you really wish you hadn't, because of the way you are looking at them.

But you are an infinitely powerful being, and it is very much within your ability to look at anything and turn it into something wonderful.

It's your interpretation of what you see that gives what you are seeing any of the power that it has.

Otherwise it has no power, because you are the creator of your physical universe and so what you see is what it becomes.

So, if you decide that your wallet and your purse and your bank account are full, even though you don't see money in them—if you decide that you are wealthy, even though you don't have any evidence to point to—Law of Attraction, being what it is—that single organizing principle of the universe—will bring you evidence of how you are right.

Because you are always right about whatever it is that you assert.

So, if you go through your day today asserting that you are wealthy, you will find evidence that that is correct.

Now, deliciously, you will also encounter the ideas

that tell you otherwise, because, as you're asserting that, you're launching new ideas, new thoughts; Law of Attraction is bringing those to you, and any thought that you have going on already that goes in the other direction—that contrasts with your new thoughts—those will become evident.

So, that's a really, really good thing, isn't it?

Because now you're going to become aware of how you don't believe that you are wealthy—or you do believe that what you're looking at is real—that the state of your wallet in the current time moment is the way it's always going to be, or it's evidence of how you're not doing it right.

As you come across those thoughts, what we recommend is that you disavow them.

We don't suggest that you push them away, because that just gives them more energy.

What we suggest is that you look at them and you say: "Yes, that's a thought that I used to think; that is a thought that I used to think, and I don't think that thought any more.

"What the thought is that I'm thinking now is that I am wealthy; that more is coming; that this situation is temporary, and that it's always getting better and better and better.

"And this old thought—it's yesterday's news.

"This is something that I used to think because I believed it, and now I don't believe it anymore.

"I can see evidence of how I did believe it, and I can feel that I believed it before; but I'm changing my

121

mind."

Now, here it may take a little bit of effort; it may take a little bit of deciding and some skill to say, "Okay, I'm not thinking that thought anymore; that's not of interest to me."

So, as you're going through your day today and you're asserting who you are in relationship to your money—which is that you are the creator; you are the one who determines what you have, and just because you don't have what you want right now doesn't mean you're doing something wrong; what it means is that this situation is temporary and it's going to be getting better and better and better—as you're doing this, and contrasting thoughts arise, you have an opportunity at every single moment—and it doesn't matter whether you take it or not; you'll get this opportunity again and again—but you have an opportunity at every single moment to decide what it is that you really want to think in this arena.

Do you really want to be focused in that way, or do you want to assert what is really true: that this is temporary?

These old thoughts, as they arise, they're not out to get you—they're not out to attack you—they're just there because you put them in place long ago.

They're there because you have a vibrational habit of thinking them, and that's all right, and we invite you to treat it as such—we invite you to treat them that way —we invite you to look at them in that lens—that it's okay that you used to think these thoughts; but the key is that you used to think them.

Because obviously you don't think them anymore, because that's why they're now presenting themselves as contrasting thoughts.

You are not interested in them anymore; they don't really have the oomph that they used to; they don't have the sway that they used to.

Now you're about asserting what you really want: "I am wealthy; I have plenty of money. More money is coming; this is temporary. I'm right here on the leading edge of my own experience, and this situation is just about the best place I've ever been."

Now, at first, some of that may seem as though you're not being completely truthful with yourself.

It may seem as though you are making it up or trying really hard to get there, and we understand that. It's those contrasting thoughts that will reinforce that idea.

But look at why you think you're telling a lie or that you're not being entirely truthful.

Most likely, it's because you're accustomed to asserting that not having money is somehow a natural state of being—and we are here to say that it's not.

Being disconnected from abundance—from your Source—is not a natural state.

A natural state is to be powerfully in the flow of who you are, and to allow whatever it is that you are wanting, in the way that you want it, to come to you.

So, as you're going through your day today and it occurs to you that perhaps you're being less than truthful with yourself, we urge you to stop and to really examine that thought, and to notice how actually incorrect it is: that you are being truthful; that abundance is your birthright—it's your natural state of being—and when you assert that you are wealthy, you are just asserting the natural state of things.

Now, what that wealth looks like to you is completely up to you.

What abundance means for you is completely up to you, and there are lots of places in your life where you already are experiencing tremendous abundance.

Previously, we invited you to look around and notice how there was a tremendous amount of abundance and wealth and money everywhere—that it really was surrounding you: all the money it took to build the things that you are living in, driving in, driving around, walking around, looking at, experiencing, hearing, feeling—all of the physical reality in your life is suffused with money.

There's just money everywhere.

So, it is everywhere, and what you're doing now is tuning into your experience of it vibrationally; and the way you do that is by asserting what it is that you want, and finding that vibration and riding it: "I am wealthy; this situation is temporary; more is coming; all is well."

And indeed it is.

124

17. Allow yourself to live as abundantly as you can

We are neither advocates of wealth nor poverty, but we do recommend that you allow yourself to live as abundantly as you possibly can; and what we mean by this is that there is no benefit to anyone, anywhere, for you to cut yourself off from the Source of All That Is.

There is no benefit to anyone, anywhere, for you to play as though you are somehow or another unable to have for yourself what it is that you're really wanting; and there is no benefit to anyone, anywhere, for you to be walking around in the idea of or in the belief that somehow or another poverty is a noble thing.

The physical universe that you inhabit is one of your own creation, and it is in this particular topic where we really want to bring home that particular point.

If this physical universe is of your own creation,

then it can be as abundant or as constricted as you prefer it to be.

Many of you have been trained by very well-meaning people to believe and to expect that your physical universe is one of lack: one where there are a limited number of resources, where there is a finite number of experiences available to you.

When you are spinning straw into gold, what you are doing is you are beginning, quite literally, with the assumption that there is an infinite amount of gold available to you.

Now, it's not really possible for you to have the experience of possessing an infinite amount of gold or money—or of really anything—but when you begin to relax into the inevitability of what it means that there is an infinite amount of resources available to you in this physical universe, then what we know is that you will experience abundance in a way that you probably cannot even really imagine from that place where you might be believing that there are a finite amount of resources.

In a physical universe with infinite resources, there is no need to grab anything.

There is no need to snatch anything away from someone else.

There is no need to pretend as though something doesn't exist in order to convince yourself that something else is a necessity.

There's no need to decide that this is something that you have to have, because if you don't have it then you are depriving yourself of something else.

In other words, many times when there is a belief in lack, what happens is you might use money—particularly money—as a way of compensating, or trying to justify whatever it is that you really do want, by saying, "Well, I can't have it because there's not enough money," or "The only way I can get it is to have a lot of money."

What we're not saying here is that you shouldn't want whatever it is that you do want.

As we said before, there is an infinite amount of everything available to you.

All that you have to do is line up with it.

In this way, what this means—in very specific and very practical terms—is that when you decide that you can have what it is that you really do want, things begin to open up for you; things begin to change for you.

You begin to find yourself not wanting things just to have them, but realizing that whatever it is that you summon forth is going to come to you; and so you can really relax into the inevitability of it, without trying so hard to make it happen in order to prove that in the midst of all of this so-called lack, that you actually can be abundant.

When you realize that there is an infinite amount of abundance available to everyone, everywhere, you don't have to hoard anything—you don't have to hold it back; you don't have to keep it tightly held in your grip —because now you are free to experience whatever it is that you want to experience; because you know that whenever you want to call upon something to come into your experience, that it will do so.

So, we invite you to go through your day today noticing the infinite amount of abundance; and if that is a difficult thing for you to conceive of, you might start with some very obvious things.

Think about how many grains of sand there are on just one beach; imagine how much water there is in the ocean; think about how much oxygen there is in the air; imagine how many blades of grass there are in a field.

Now, these things that we're mentioning, they are finite, but the numbers are so large that they might as well be infinite; because if you were to count all the grains of sand just on one beach, you would spend so much time counting it that it would take what would seem like forever.

If you tried to measure the ocean one teaspoon at a time, you would find yourself counting until most likely the end of time, if there were to be such a thing.

Imagine the number of stars that are actually in the sky; not the ones that you can see, but the ones that you can't see.

Imagine how many seconds you've been alive.

As you think about these things—as you think about these very, very large-quantity things—you will begin to understand how much there actually is.

We cannot convince you of infinite abundance, but what we can do is suggest—as we are doing so here—that you spend some time contemplating things that are very large in quantity.

Law of Attraction will bring you more and more evidence of how much there is of so many things; and that is our goal here today: to invite you to cultivate the thought of what an infinite abundance would be.

You can't really conceive of it; but you can find evidence of its possibility in all sorts of places, and just thinking about those things that we mentioned today will bring you more and more ideas about how large infinite actually might be.

18. The thought that feels better arises naturally from within you

The next step on any journey is always the thought that feels better; and this thought that feels better arises naturally from within you.

We like to call this following your intuition, because the thought that feels better is the one that is the next point of vibrational expansion that you are capable of reaching right from where you are.

There is a reason why we come back to this topic again and again.

And it is because the thought that feels better—the one that you can reach from right where you are—is the one that is telling you, "This is the next step."

This is the thing that will bring you closer and closer—that is leading you to—that will cause you to have what it is that you are wanting—what it is that you've been dreaming; because all of the desires that you have launched must come home to you.

And every desire that you have launched—assembled in the way that is just perfect from where you are, for you—is calling you forth through this expanded vibrational state.

It is natural and normal for you to have the wanted aspect of anything that you are thinking about, even when you have a very mixed vibration—even when you're not sure that you can have what it is that you want.

By following the thought that feels better right from where you are, what you are doing is literally walking into the wanted aspect of the very best possible thing—experience, situation, possibility, relationship—that you can have; and this right here is the very key to spinning straw into gold.

By following your intuition in this way, you are doing two things simultaneously:

One is, you are positioning yourself to be exactly at the right place at the right time for all that you are asking for.

The second is that you are just feeling better; and—as we've said before—feeling better is its own reward in the sense that as you feel better things get better, and the better things get the better you feel, and the better you feel the better things get, on and on like this.

So, as you follow your intuition day by day, moment by moment—as it is your intuition to follow your intuition, as it is your intention to reach for thoughts that feel better from right where you are, as it is your intention to speak only the words that feel better right from where you are, as it is your intention to only do that which feels better in its doing right from where you are—you will notice very quickly, as you make a practice of this, how much better circumstances in your life become.

So, if you have decided that you are wanting to create money, and if you have decided that you are wanting to master the art of creating money, and if you have decided that abundance and well-being and wealth in a manner of ways is your inheritance and your birthright and is something that not only you can have but that you are destined to have—not because there is a destiny waiting for you, but because of all of the massive rockets of desire that you have launched in the past for more and more of this really good stuff—once you have decided these things—and they're not difficult things to decide—once you have decided these things, as you are following the thought that feels better, you will find yourself arriving in situations and experiences that reinforce these beliefs very quickly.

In fact, in a matter of hours in one day, if you were to be persistent in following the thought that feels better, you would find yourself in vastly improved circumstances that would reinforce your vastly improved vibration very, very quickly.

So we invite you today to really—with intention and with a little bit of perseverance and persistence—to follow the thoughts that feel better.

Now, the very first thing that we want to say about that is that as you are doing this, part of what you will be sorting out is the difference between the thought that feels better because it feels better right now, and the thought that feels better because of what you think it will bring you later.

This is the difference, in essence, between wanting and having.

When you are accustomed to not having and to not even wanting, wanting is actually a really wonderful thing; because when you are saying, "I want this and I want this and I want this," what you're doing is you're opening up your mind to new possibilities, to things that you hadn't considered before.

But as you go along, at some point you're going to want to change your wanting into having.

As you go along, there's going to be a point where you're going to want to say—instead of "I want this"— you're going to want to say, "I have it."

But only if it feels better to do so.

We imagine that, quite quickly as you practice finding thoughts that feel better, one of the things that you will notice is that it does feel better to state that you have something, rather than you want it.

There's nothing wrong with saying you want it— and sometimes that is the thought that feels better—but sometimes the thought that feels better is a much more radical statement: one that is much more ambitious in its scope, which is to say, "I have it."

And, notice that we're not saying that you're proving yourself right by doing this; what we're saying is, that's just the thought that feels better; but it will prove you right.

The difference here between wanting something and having something is that wanting it means that you will have it later, and having it means that you have it now.

Now, we're not saying that you actually physically can possess this thing—whatever it is that you are wanting—or that the quality or the experience has come to you, necessarily, right in that red-hot minute.

But as you are asserting that, Law of Attraction—being what it is, of course—will bring it to you.

Again, the practice today is not to tell the difference between wanting and having; but we're bringing that up because—very quickly when you are following the thought that feels better—it will become obvious that there is a vast difference between thinking a thought that feels better because of what you think it will bring you later, and thinking a thought that feels better because it literally just feels better right now—and there's nothing more important than improving your vibration right from where you are.

There's nothing more important than feeling better right in this moment.

Another way of thinking about it is: there's nothing more important than flowing downstream with all that you are—and that is what these better-feeling thoughts are doing.

They are leading you downstream; they are the downstream thoughts.

The other wonderful thing about this practice is that you know in an instant—you know immediately—whether or not you are feeling better.

It's not something that you have to wait for and see: How did that work out? or What is going to happen then? or How is that thing actually working?

You know immediately whether it works or not.

The trick here is to realize that you can feel better all the time, from everywhere that you are.

There is always a slightly better vibrational stance from any vibrational stance that you might be in.

When you are suffused with joy and freedom and abundance and love and all of those things which mean pretty much the same thing—which is, you are really plugged in and connected to Source Energy, to your Inner Being, your Higher Self—when you are in that place, you're constantly moving towards slightly improved vibrational states that just keep getting a little bit better and a little better.

And so, it might seem like nothing is really happening—you just feel really, really good—but a whole lot is happening.

No matter what is going on—no matter what you are feeling, no matter where you are vibrationally—when you are finding thoughts that feel better, you are going downstream; you are moving in the direction of who you really are; you are finding yourself eventually —if not immediately—but eventually in your vortex:

that place where you really are plugged in and tuned in to your Inner Being, that place where you are in the most important relationship and are focused on the most important relationship in your life, which is the one with your Inner Being, Source Energy in manifestation.

As you follow in this direction, you will find that conditions improve, situations improve, relationships improve.

You will find that you are more relaxed and more open and more allowing than perhaps you have been in quite a while, even if you are quite accustomed to being allowing and open and receiving.

You will find that you are taking action that feels really delicious; you will find that you are speaking words that feel really good to say, right when you're saying them.

You will find that everything looks a little bit better; everything feels a little bit better; everything tastes a little bit better.

This isn't nirvana. This is your natural state.

This isn't some place that you're going to go and visit for a little while; this is a place that is normal for you to be in, and that is endlessly fascinating and endlessly interesting and endlessly expansive.

From where you're sitting, it might seem like it's not that interesting and it might get boring after a while; but we guarantee you that that is not the case, because there is always an expanded vibrational state from where you are.

137

It's only the narrowness of your imagination in a constricted space that would ever say that joy could be boring—and it's okay.

Just follow one thought that feels better from where you are.

Don't worry about trying to figure out what's going to happen later, because that's not really a thought that feels better right now from where you are, most likely.

The thoughts that feel better from where you are just simply feel better.

They don't seem to be going anywhere specific, yet they are expanding into a much bigger place; and Law of Attraction—being what it is—will actually match you up with wanted aspects of all manner of things as you are becoming more and more of a vibrational match to them.

So, today can be a very delicious day, just like every day, if you allow yourself to have it; and as you go through the day reaching for thoughts that feel better, we invite you to just revel in it and to bask in it and to milk it and to notice—every time that a thought feels better—how you are in a slightly more expanded vibrational state, and to realize that this is your natural state.

It's highly unnatural to be planning, to be strategizing, to be trying to figure out what is next and what you're supposed to do and where to go and how to do it.

It's highly natural to follow the flow of your own powerful desires—a very, very powerful flow that is leading you to more and more of what you are wanting more and more of.

Not just things—it's also leading you to states of being, qualities of relationships, experiences and situations.

So as you follow all of this today, and you find thoughts that feel better right from where you are, we know that you will remember that this really is exactly how you spin straw into gold, right in the moment.

And we are very much looking forward to hearing all about your delicious stories and how things have gotten better and better, for we know that, as you practice this, they will, very clearly and very quickly.

19. There is within you a single creative power

There is within you a single power—and that power is given many different names—but it is a creative power that is ultimately creative: that cannot be used for any other purpose than creation; it does not destroy, it only expands; it only evolves.

You can call it love; you can call it joy; you can call it freedom; you can call it Source Energy in manifestation; you can call it Source Energy in action.

It doesn't really matter how you think about it or what name you give it.

There is a single power for expansion that is always flowing through you and that is always available to you.

The way you harness this power is through your imagination and your focus.

The way this power expands is through that which you call Law of Attraction—that single organizing prin-

141

ciple of the universe.

The way in which this power manifests is through your allowing.

It is natural and normal for any idea that you summon forth to come into manifested reality exactly—exactly—in the way that you have summoned it forth to do so.

There is no lack in your universe; there is no lack in your experience.

This creative power did not create something unwanted; that is only your perspective, and as you change your mind about what you are seeing and about what you are experiencing, you will discover the profound abundance that exists in all places, in all things, in all ways.

All that is really needed—all that is really being asked for, as you are learning over and over again—specifically with spinning straw into gold, developing mastery over the art of creating money—all that is happening is that you are turning your attention again and again back to this same power that flows through you.

This power is not located inside your body. It is not located in any specific place.

It actually is everywhere.

It is in everything that you touch, it is in everything that you can see, and it is in everything that you imagine.

When you are in touch with this power—by that we mean when you are allowing it to flow through unimpeded—you can feel it, because you feel yourself being carried by it.

Some have referred to this experience as flowing downstream: a metaphor that we really very much like.

When you are allowing what is natural and normal for you to express itself, you will feel as though you are being carried downstream by a very powerful river, and this river is the sum total of all of the desires that you have brought forth into manifestation through the ideas that you have given birth to.

Not every single thing that you have ever had a desire for has come forth into manifestation.

Those things that are not physically present are metaphysically present in what we like to refer to as your vibrational warehouse.

There, the wanted aspect of everything you have ever given birth to through ideas, through thoughts, through the rockets of desire that you have launched, are waiting for you to become a vibrational match to them.

There are many, many more things in this vibrational warehouse than you could ever experience in a thousand years of being alive.

But everything that is there you will become a match to.

Most of it you will become a match to when you find yourself transitioning from where you are physically back into your non-physical state.

In other words, when you die you will experience everything that is in your vibrational warehouse; but you will only experience it from the wanted aspect of everything.

We remind you of this because we want you to understand that there's really no rush to get anything or to do anything or to have anything.

However, you don't have to wait until you die to feel that sense of powerful fulfillment and satisfaction.

That's available to you right now.

It doesn't come to you just because you croak; it comes to you because you decide you can have what you really want.

And that is a very, very powerful thing indeed to be going back to, over and over again: to be saying to yourself, "I can have what it is that I'm really wanting."

And that is the thing that we invite you to experience today as you're going through your day: to look around—not at what you don't have—but to look around and notice what is on its way, to notice what is incipient in manifestation, to notice what is imminent and inevitable; because it is coming.

What you are wanting—what you have given your attention to and what you are cultivating a vibration towards—is coming to you.

it is coming to you all of the time you care, constantly manifesting; and as you realize that that is going on—that you are the reason why the physical universe around you exists, and you are the only reason that it exists—when you realize that, you will begin to understand more and more each and every day how inevitably what you are wanting—particularly those things that you consider to be very important—are coming to you.

Your only job is to line up with its inevitability; and for many of you, most of the time but not always, that's going to feel like allowing what it is that you are wanting to come into your experience.

There's no trick here; there's no process or technique that is going to be the one thing that makes everything that you want happen.

There is, however, the decision that you can have it; and as you go through your day today, we invite you to turn to that decision again and again and again and just notice whether you have made that decision, or if there is something somewhere that you have decided that you can't have because of conditions or situations or circumstances.

And every time you come across one of those thoughts, we do invite you to think, "Is that really true? Is there something that is keeping me from having this? And if there is, what is it?"

And what you will notice again and again is that, while some of it may be situational and you're thinking, "Well, this has to happen before I can have that," most of what you will notice is that it's just the way that you think, and you can change your mind.

You may not feel as though you can do that immediately, but you can change your mind on anything that you want to.

It's always possible to go from a place of contraction or lack to a place of abundance and expansion.

So, as you're going through your day today and

you're noticing all of these wonderful aspects of who you are, and you're noticing that this is exactly right—that you are in the right place at the right time and that this day is unfolding perfectly—and you're asking yourself the question, "Can I really have what it is that I really want?" and you notice whether or not you have made that decision, we know that by turning your attention in these directions, you are inevitably becoming a match to more and more and more of what you are wanting, and you're no longer walking through your experience as though you were asleep.

You are now opening your eyes to what you have created, what you are creating, what is coming, and what you are becoming as a result.

20. Contrast is always helping you

Contrast arises naturally in every situation, no matter what it is that you are thinking about or where it is that you are pointing your focus of concentration consciousness.

It's very important to remember, as you're spinning straw into gold, that contrast is actually helping you define and refine what it is that you are wanting.

If you did not have contrast, if you did not have those thoughts arising—either in manifested form or just in the ideas of them—that were showing you how you didn't want to go in the direction you were pointing in, then you would not understand the value of or be able to keenly define what it is that you're really wanting.

We understand why it would be very, very delicious —in concept at least—to live a life where there was very little contrast whatsoever.

But what we want to remind you is that it is the contrast of your experience that has actually helped you over and over and over again to come very clearly into alignment with what you are really wanting.

You have been living your life for as long as you've been living it, and, for however long you've been living it, most likely you've been either avoiding contrast or you've been trying to put it off, or you've been trying to fix it, or you've been trying to manage it in some way.

As you become more and more allowing of all of your experiences by turning your attention to what feels better, moment after moment after moment, what you will begin to notice is that contrast doesn't need to be managed.

There's nothing wrong with it, and so it doesn't need to be fixed.

There's nothing bad about it, and so it doesn't need to be resisted or avoided in any way.

Contrast is arising to tell you that you have two different thoughts on the same topic: one is going in one direction and one is going in another; and when you are addressing those thoughts and you are saying, "All right, I'm going to bring my attention to the one that feels better—to the one that I like the best—and I'm going to allow the other one to be what it is," what happens is the conflict that was engendered in the contrast suddenly disappears, because the thought that is no longer useful or helpful goes on its way and moves on.

It goes on its way because you've withdrawn your

attention from it, and you are no longer trying to make it be something other than what it is.

As you're going through your day today, we invite you to be aware of contrast as it arises, and to—instead of trying to fix it or change it or manifest it in some other form or manage it in some way or turn it around or heal it, or whatever it is that you might normally be doing—we recommend that you just allow it to be what it is.

When you stop for a moment and you say, "I'm okay with this, even though I don't like it"—because we're not suggesting that you like what arises that you don't like; what we're suggesting is that you find a way to be okay with it just by allowing it to be what it is; and when you do this—when you say, "I'm okay with the contrast that has arisen here, and I'm okay with the way that this is sorting itself out, and I'm okay with the fact that I have two different ideas on the same subject"— what you're doing is you're withdrawing any attention or power or alignment that you've given to the contrasting thought, and you're bringing your focus completely to the thought that feels better in that situation.

So, if you've decided that you are wealthy, and you've made that powerful decision and you're going along finding thoughts that feel better, and what arises is the thought that, No, you're not wealthy, you're actually in dire straits and you'd better do something or else, what you'll become aware of is that you have two different thoughts on the same idea:

The idea that you're wealthy is just a declaration of

your relationship to your finances, or to money, or to the having of money, or whatever it may mean specifically for you.

The contrasting thought that arises says to you, "No, that's not the case."

The thought that you've been following that felt better said, "Yes, it is the case."

So, you've got two conflicting thoughts on the same subject: one that says no and one that says yes.

You are the one who is creating your reality, and you are the one who is deciding what is true; so you get at that moment to decide which one is true.

Now, the problem here for most of our physical friends is that the thought that says no—you've been trained to believe that there might be some truth to that, so you better do something about it.

What we're suggesting here is that there is no truth to it; it's just a conflicting thought—and just because it conflicts doesn't mean there's anything you have to do about it, other than just to allow it to be what it is.

So, as you do this, what will happen is that the thought will just move on, and you'll go back to the thought that you've been thinking all along, which is, "I am wealthy, yes I am. I am wealthy and all is well"— whatever thought feels better from where you are in that instance.

If, instead, what you had done is you had stopped and tried to manage that thought that said no, that you are not wealthy, and gave you all sorts of evidence or reasons why that's not the case—if you had stopped and tried to manage that thought, you would have become entangled in it; and being entangled in it you would have started generating evidence as to how it was actually true.

Now, here's one thing to remember: if you get entangled in it, it's not a big deal either.

All that happens there is that you just experience more of something that you probably have already experienced quite a bit of in the past.

Most of these contrasting thoughts are not really new; they're just kind of like the greatest hits from the past that keep arising over and over again.

But if you were to get entangled in it, then all you have to do at any moment is decide, "Okay, what I would really rather do here is find a thought that feels better"; and you always have that opportunity.

It's never too late to make that choice.

You're never really doing anything but delaying the experience you want. You're not missing the experience—you're just delaying it.

So, even if you were to become entangled in a contrasting thought as it arises, as you're asserting some new reality that you're creating, we would suggest not to worry about it too much—not to make it such a big deal, not to even really, necessarily report on it to your neighbor, to your friends, to your colleagues—to just really notice, "All right, that's a contrasting thought that has arisen and that's all right. I'm okay with that, and I got tangled up in it a little bit and I fought it for a while—I tried to fix it, I tried to manage it, I tried to make things better because of my belief that the contrasting thought was correct—but what I really want is to feel better; because I know that in feeling better, conditions will change and they will improve and they will line up with the thoughts that I'm asserting, and that's what I really want."

So, as you make this decision, what you will notice is that you get back on track: the contrasting thought will go on its way, evolving into whatever it is to become, and you will find yourself more and more in alignment with what you are asserting.

Now, as you go through your day today and you're noticing how this works and what happens as contrasting thoughts arise, again, we do suggest that you be very, very easy with yourself.

If you feel the need to fix it, then by all means go in and fix it and see what happens. See what happens when you get entangled with it.

We think you will be quite interested to notice how subtle it is when you are getting involved in these thoughts that do not feel better—thoughts that feel worse.

If you haven't really closely paid attention to this before, as you're going through the day today you might be quite surprised at how subtle the change is.

It's still present, but you might think, "Well, I've never really noticed this before"—but today, as you're paying attention, you will begin to notice and have more awareness about why contracting thoughts feel worse.

152

The goal for today, if you will, is to understand why the thought that feels better really is the thought that feels better; why the thought that feels better leads to what you want more of; and why dealing with—messing with, fixing, changing, sorting out, rearranging—contrasting thoughts doesn't always work the way you think it's going to.

Now, what we know about this experience—what we know will happen is this:

We don't know specifically what you will do or what you will experience; but what we do know is that as you become more and more aware of thoughts that feel better and why they feel better and why that is helpful and why that is useful and why that is worthy of your attention, what we know is that as you go through this day today you will find yourself experiencing changes in your conditions, probably more rapidly than you have noticed thus far to date.

We're not saying that everything will become perfect; what we are saying is that you will notice the improvements much quicker than you might have noticed them before.

When you set out today with that expectation—that everything is going to get better, that you are going to follow the thoughts that feel better and you're going to do so with great ease and without making it a really big deal, but just going in that direction generally, over and over again, as and when you remember to do so—that you're going to allow contrasting thoughts to just be what they are, to be okay with them even though you

153

don't like them, even though you don't really want to line up with them, to just let them be what they are—as you follow these things, what we notice and what we expect is that you will find yourself experiencing greater and greater, wondrously delicious experiences that continue to expand and that do so under your very nose, and you will see things that have always been going on but that you might not have ever really paid attention to.

So, we are looking forward to how delicious this day will be for you, and we are very much looking forward to all of the ways in which these manifested ideas that we are bringing forth here play out in your wonderful life, and we are very much looking forward to knowing that you are having exactly what it is that you are wanting today.

21. There is no limit to what you can have

There is no limit to what you can have; all that is necessary is that you decide what it is that you're wanting and allow yourself to have it.

When we say this, what we are saying is that all of the limits that you have to your experience are self-imposed.

None of them are coming to you from the outside; no one is holding you back, even if that's the way it looks to you.

What we want you to remember as you go through your day today is that everything that you want is available to you, and that your ability to experience anything is limitless.

It is important to remember, however, that you may not be able to experience everything that you are wanting immediately from where you are, because it is

155

a vibrational game.

And so, as you are following what feels better, what you are doing is literally following the vibrational path that will bring you to the very best of what you are wanting in the very best way possible in the most efficient way that there is.

And so, spinning straw into gold is deciding what it is that you are wanting, deciding that you can have it, and following what feels better from where you are.

And as you do this, literally you are shaping—defining and refining—everything that you are experiencing.

It's not just about money; but in the topic of money —in that arena—what we want you to remember as you go through the day today is that you really can have everything that you are wanting.

So, as you walk through your day, we invite you to notice what it is that you really do want.

Many of you have become so accustomed to not having what it is that you are wanting that it may take a little while for you to realize what it is that you specifically want in the arena of money.

Some of you are very, very clear and know exactly what it is that you're wanting; and some of you are somewhere in between, having a vague idea of what it is that you want more of, but not really clear about what that might be and not really having given yourself the time and the attention to refine and define what that might be and how you want to experience it.

Now, it is important to remember that as you are thinking about this, and as you are discovering what it is that you are wanting more and more of, it's not your job to figure out how you're going to get there from where you are.

That's the job of Law of Attraction, the single, organizing principle of the universe.

It's not necessary for you to know, or to even understand how it is that you're going to go from here to there.

One of the things that you can count on, however, is that it will be a vibrational journey first and foremost.

Action will be involved, no doubt; but first it will be vibration—and first, by following what feels better, you will move progressively from where you are into the vibrational space of having and allowing what it is that you are wanting.

It's really quite simple in this way.

Since you are a vibrational being in a vibrational universe, having vibrational experiences that are manifested into physical reality, everything that you want and everything that you are becoming, everything that you are thinking of and everything that you are experiencing is all vibrational in nature.

So, your job is just to become a match to what it is that you are wanting; and the fastest, most efficient way to do this, of course, is to follow the thought that feels better from where you are, to say those words that feel better in their speaking, and to do those things that feel better in their doing.

We want to remind you that as you are following what feels better, what you will not be doing is doing things because of what it will bring you later.

What you will be doing is noticing just what feels better right in the moment.

This is why we have said, again and again, there's no reason to wait to feel better from where you are.

There's no reason to do something that feels worse because of what you think it will bring you later, because that never really works out the way that you think it's going to.

What we most want you to remember as you go through the day today is that as you're following the thought that feels better, and as you're exploring the idea of what it is that you really do want on the topic of money, that there really is no limit.

We'll say this again and again and again, because it does bear repeating.

It is somewhat built into you—for reasons that are very cultural in nature and that come from very well-meaning, well-intentioned people in your past—that you can only have a certain amount, or a certain limit, or a certain range of experiences when it comes to money.

And so, as you are going through the day today and you become aware of that, we invite you to not try to bust through those walls, but rather to just lean into slightly expanded versions of them; and if you do that, moment by moment, very quickly you will move into a much broader, much bigger expectation of what is possible.

But if you're trying to bust down those walls and

kick down those walls and get rid of them, it probably will get all tangled up—and what you really don't want to do here is to add any further resistance to the topic of money.

So, as you're going through the day and as you're thinking about what it is that you're wanting, when you lean into the future and follow the thought that feels better from where you are, what you will notice is that it's a lot easier to expand your notion of what it is that you can have by just relaxing into where you are—by just taking a deep breath and finding yourself once again expecting a little bit more and a little bit more and a little bit more.

And, very quickly—just in a few moments really, if you do that with some persistence—you will find that you have really opened up a whole world of possibilities that had not even occurred to you just moments before.

But it's not because you pushed into it.

It's because you relaxed into it. It's because you eased your way into it.

So, this day—this final day on this very delicious topic of spinning straw into gold—we invite you to expect it to be truly, truly remarkable and truly, truly wonderful.

We invite you to think about all of the ways in which you can have more and more of what it is that you're truly wanting on the topic of money.

It might surprise you to discover what feels like real wealth—what feels like real abundance on this particular topic.

You might be accustomed to looking at cultural images of wealth and abundance and assuming that that's what it is that you're wanting, because that's what everyone else appears to be having—and we're not saying you shouldn't want those things.

What we are saying is that there is a very, very personal, very intimate and very powerful version of abundance that you are calling forth.

It doesn't require a lot of effort on your part to expand these ideas of what you can have.

It doesn't requite a lot of effort on your part to relax into these more expanded versions.

It might take a little bit of persistence in realizing that you don't have to figure it out, but rather that the idea of an expanded version of abundance is actually trying to get to you already, because of the massive rockets of desire that you have launched in the past around this very, very delicious topic.

Epilogue

The universal organizing principle, based in love, is unconditional in how it perceives you.

It cares not what you think; for it knows that you, as a master manifestor and powerful creator,know exactly what you are doing.

It trusts you explicitly.

It does not try to control you, to fix you, to manipulate you, or to get you to be good.

It cannot imagine you as anything less than unconditional love.

So, whatever you give focus to must expand.

That is the nature of creation.

If you take a thought and hold it clearly in your mind

for a few seconds, you can test the validity of what we are saying.

You will begin to notice, after a few seconds of clear and focused thinking, that new thoughts will begin to come to you about whatever you are focused upon.

This is the organizing principle in action.

Now, why does it take a few seconds for this to happen?

Well, part of the blended reality you have come into as a physical being includes the concept of time.

Time is just the way that you use to organize your experiences while you are here in physical focus.

It is not immutable, and is more like a filing system that you use in a busy office to organize information that would otherwise be chaotic and difficult to understand.

Imagine, however, if you started a religion from your filing system.

Imagine that you began to say that this is how everyone should organize their lives.

Then you get a glimpse into the power that you all give this stream of time.

You all believe that everything has a beginning, a middle, and an end.

Those things that you like seem to end too quickly, and those things that you don't like seem to linger on endlessly.

Neither is really true—not at the level of consciousness.

But your experience of them is very real and based on how you bring your focus to your life.

When you begin to relax a bit about these beliefs around time, you might notice that things seem to improve a bit.

You might notice, in fact, that time is really your friend,

and not the enemy you may have made it out to be.

Like everything, your relationship to time is based on how you perceive and the thoughts you consistently think about it.

The organizing principle of the Universe brings you more and more of what you are noticing, and you get consistent proof of how what you are perceiving is correct.

And isn't that a wonderful thing!

Acknowledgments

This is going to be long. Just so you know.

How this particular book came about in practical terms is pretty simple. In late December of 2011 I let folks know that I would be hosting a daily morning conversation series on the topic of Spinning Straw Into Gold. Twenty-five hardy souls signed up and you have just read what happened next.

So, my first thanks go to those wonderful people who were part of this conversation series. Their energy, ideas, contrast, and desires brought forth these ideas. To all of you: many, many thanks for your delicious presence!

I would not be doing this work, in the way that I'm doing it, if it were not for Martin Jurow telling my wonderfully wise mother that she had to get Shirley MacLaine's latest book: *Out on a Limb.*

My mother then told me that I should read it. Being 19, I, of course, did not.

Then I met a man in 1986 who told me the exact same thing and, so, of course, I did! I would have jumped off a bridge if he had suggested it. You know who you are. Thank you is really not enough, but it will have to suffice.

Not long after I discovered the Seth Material and bought every copy I could get my hands on. *Out on a Limb* was made into a TV movie, and I saw Kevin Ryerson and Sture Johansson channeling on my television and knew there was something going on that I wanted to be part of.

The book *Opening to Channel* was the device that got me to that place I was looking for in early 1990. Many thanks to Sanaya Roman and Duane Packer for producing the very best book on the subject.

My experience as a channel evolved over the years, including a stint for 10 years in the so-called "real world" holding down a corporate job and being miserable most of the time.

During that period of stops and starts and exploration, many, many people showed up to show me the way. A few of them that I want to say special thanks to (in order of appearance) are Billy Cross, the guys in the corner at the NYC Healing Circle, Gregg Cassin, Matt Wick, Karen Divine (yes, I know!), Maria Martinez, Scott Fowler, Deb Mangelus, Amy Roberts, the gang in Provincetown that winter, Virginia Loridans and the gang in Shreveport that summer, Sherry & James Ramsey, Margaret Levering, Stacy Jackson, Chris May, Brad Newell, and Brent Almond & Nick Pirulli.

During a vacation to Guerneville, California, in August of 2005, something extraordinary happened. After 10 years of being involved in trying valiantly and stubbornly to insert a square peg in a round hole, I suddenly remembered that I didn't have to. Very special thanks to Masada for your healing touch and strong intuition that woke me from my long sleep and reminded me that I really, really love to talk and how that was totally fine.

Once I knew I had to go, I turned to Doug Upchurch and told him as much and found great wisdom in his loving friendship and powerful coaching.

To the amazing Austin friends who watched me lose the Mercedes (then the Toyota!), sell practically everything I owned, and turn my life upside-down. Thank you for your love and friendship and for staying the course with me: David Cobb (another powerful coach!), Jason Morris (your book is next!), Marcie & Derek Joñez (and Master Harrison!), and particularly Tyler Reeves (Iconoclasts-R-Us!).

In the middle of my re-awakening, I somehow moved to Dallas. This is where the moment where everything changed happened. One night, after dinner, it seemed like I was supposed to channel for my dear friend Paul Labar. That's the night I first "met" the non-physical Paul and The Communion of Light, although I didn't know much about them (or that I had already met them). I also got to meet Paul's mother that night, which was very sweet!

Much to my surprise, I found an amazing group of

people in Fort Worth who were studying the teachings of Abraham. Thanks to all of you for helping me re-emerge as a channel and for being so much fun to hang out with!

During my spiritual pilgrimage to Dallas, Lori Archibald, Leza Isadora, and Robin Newland provided all manner of support, material and otherwise. Lori and Robin made sure I went to that Abraham workshop in San Antonio where I saw someone else doing the same thing I was doing, That was a huge eye-opener.

Thank you Carole and Phil Layman for hosting the very first Communion of Light sessions in Arlington.

Once I got back to Austin, C. introduced me to a powerful group of creators. We had quite a ride and I'm beyond grateful for all the support that was shared over those amazing months. Thanks for asking me how you could help me with this work and then delivering on two great workshops!

Now, there are a whole heck of a lot of people that I want to mention specifically for the pivotal roles each of them had in helping me refine and define my work with Paul. But it's not my place to talk about my clients (that just never feels right), so let me generally say:

Thanks to the early "regular regulars," all of whom are still around. Many thanks particularly to K. and M. for helping me shape the nature of my business.

Thank you to everyone in The Village. Your questions and your desires have given birth to so much rich insight, it's quite astounding to even think about.

On the road, I have been blessed to connect with a

wonderful array of folks as I've taken COL workshops all over the US and Canada. Every workshop has been my favorite: Albany, Ottawa, Montreal, NYC, Austin, Long Island, Providence, Dallas, Denver, Santa Fe, Salt Lake City (yes, 2 people is a workshop!), Burlington, and Montpelier. Can't wait to see you all again!

Thank you Judy and Michel Marcellot for the pizza, the lotions, and the magic.

Thank you Laura Gevanter for the spot coaching and for texting me whenever you see the Countess in the Hamptons.

Thank you Matt O'Grady for providing support in all sorts of astonishing ways.

Thank you Jeannette Maw for bringing me into your Good Vibe University and giving me an early place to share Paul's voice. And thank you for showing me that playing and having fun are some of the best tools for creating money!

Thank you Adrienne Melton for saying, "I know you're doing the right thing," even when it was not at all apparent that this was the case.

Thank you Flavia Daay for more than space allows.

Thank you to Belinda and Michael Morris for helping give birth to the early versions of this book. Thanks Michael for transcribing the Prologue!

Also, thank you Belinda and Michael, and Vickie and Donny Greenway for your amazing talents in producing the 2011 Texas workshops. Delicious is the only word that applies here!

Thank you to the miniature horses who liked me as

long as I had a treat to give them and whose humans, Barry and Kathy, kindly provided me a wonderful spot to spend the summer out in the country, where I could stand in the warm breeze late at night and wonder at all the stars in the sky.

Thank you Dennis Tardan and Melissa Roth for, literally, everything. Words really can't say enough.

Thank you Chip Engelmann for helping me discover Ventura County, your powerful coaching, and all of your help in so many ways. Cowabunga!

Thank you Julie Bernstein Engelmann for the glorious and divine editing (all mistakes are mine). She's also a divine artist. You can see her breathtaking abstract paintings at www.julieengelmann.com.

Thank you to that anonymous angel who called and said, "What will it take to get this first book done?" Thank you, thank you, thank you!

Thanks to my family for all your love and support all the while.

Thanks to my mother, Carol Haggard, who has been open to and aware of this remarkable path since the very beginning and, while I know she probably sometimes rolls her eyes at it some of what happens, she's very sweet to never do it in front of me.

Thank you B.L.B. for remaining (mostly) calm while all this happened. I love you very dearly.

Thank you Jane Roberts for writing your psychic manifesto. Thank you Robert Butts for all your notes.

And, thank you Esther Hicks for creating a new language and for going first.

About Frank Butterfield

Frank Butterfield is a master channel who has helped thousands experience powerful shifts in consciousness through his delicious work with The Communion of Light, a group of non-physical beings who speak through him using a single voice.

Paul, as this voice is called, shares a consistent and powerful message of freedom that we create our reality and are not at the effect of it, that we can joyfully remember who we really are as these creators, and that life comes together much simpler and easier than we've taught ourselves to believe.

Frank travels internationally, sharing Paul's voice with groups and individuals, in person and online.

For more information:

communionoflight.com

Paul & the Communion of Light on Facebook:

facebook.com/CommunionOfLight

17502295R00101

Made in the USA
Lexington, KY
18 September 2012